Days of

FRANCE

Days out in
FRANCE

Geoffrey Hindley

Columbus Books
London

Line illustrations feature the Quai aux Herbes, Ghent (page 26); the Grosse Horloge, Rouen (page 42); the Abbaye aux Hommes, Caen (page 49); La Lieutenance, Honfleur (page 56); La Maison des Plaids, Dol (page 70); the ramparts and the Tour Nichot, Fougères (page 72); Mont-St-Michel (page 74); the Cour d'Honneur of the Hôtel-Dieu, Beaune (page 84); the west front of the Cathedral, Chartres (page 87); the Place François Rude, Dijon (page 88); the main front seen from the ornamental entrance gate, Fontainebleau (page 92); the Arche des Grands-Près (or Porte d'Eau), Vendôme (page 98); the Valentré Bridge, Cahors (page 114); the Porte Cadène, St Émilion (page 116); the main square, Arles (page 122); Romanesque cloister, Aix-en-Provence (page 126); the Pont-du-Gard (Roman aqueduct), Nîmes (page 140); the Negresco Hôtel, Nice (page 155).

First published in Great Britain in 1988 by
Columbus Books Limited
19-23 Ludgate Hill, London EC4M 7PD

Designed by Pat Craddock
Line illustrations by Cathy May
Sketch maps by author

British Library Cataloguing in Publication Data
Hindley, Geoffrey, 1935-
    Days out in France.
    1. France—Description and travel—1975-
    —Guide-books
    I. Title
    914.4'04838   DC29.3

    ISBN 0–86287–319–3

Phototypeset by Falcon Graphic Art Ltd
Wallington, Surrey
Printed and bound by
The Guernsey Press, Guernsey, CI

CONTENTS

INTRODUCTION

This is not a guidebook to France in the generally accepted sense, as a glance at the contents page will soon reveal. No attempt is made to provide a survey of the whole country. Instead I have taken some of the most popular centres on the holidaymaker's itinerary and tried to indicate the possibilities these offer the traveller with a day to spare. The aim is to extend horizons, not to map the terrain.

Nor is this a book exclusively for the motorist. The excellent rail network serves the day-tripper well. In fact, two or three of the excursions proposed would be impossible without the high-speed TGV trains. Spending a family holiday in the Camargue, the adventurous can plan a lunch at Lyon, the gastronomic capital of the world (so the Lyonnais claim). From Paris, Dijon – capital of the burgundy wine region – is a comfortable day-trip distant. But car-drivers *are* invited to be enterprising. The mysterious stones of Carnac, though on the other side of the peninsula, are a perfectly feasible long day-trip from St Malo, just as Mont-St-Michel is from Caen. And how many visitors realize that Bruges and Ghent, two of northern Europe's most beautiful towns, are a manageable distance for a return journey from Calais?

In my selections I have aimed for variety – a day in the forests near Alençon; the vintage car museum at Rennes; the unexpected charms of Vendôme. The classics are not forgotten – Reims; Fontainebleau; Mont-St-Michel itself. Where there is good shopping I have tried to point it out. History, with particular reference to English connections, is given its due. This is not a gastronomic guide, but where food is the objective I have suggested the occasional restaurant. Some trips are a day's expedition, others a short journey to a great building or delightful beach. Throughout I have tried to be specific (and accurate!) in route directions, to help you plan the journey on your road map. A couple of the suggested trips are mini-tours and here there are sketch maps in the text.

The book is divided by section according to the points of departure: the various Channel ports; the capital, Paris; Bergerac for the Dordogne; Arles for the Camargue; and St Raphael and St Tropez for the Riviera. Since most of these towns are themselves worthy of attention they too have detailed descriptions – all except Paris. An eighteenth-century traveller once claimed that with the help of a racing phaeton, thoroughbred horses and the minimum of attention to building interiors, he had 'done' Rome between sunrise and sunset on a spring day. You can try to match this record for Paris if you will, but without my help.

As it is, you may decide to be selective about what to visit even from the options I have picked out for some of the great cities such as Rouen or Avignon. But whether your idea of enjoyment is a packed programme based on a strict timetable or a more leisurely itinerary with plenty of time for dawdling, watching the world go by from a pavement café or exploring the range and breadth of restaurant menus, you will find a wealth of possibilities in the pages that follow.

How to use this book

Each destination entry is headed by the recommended route; the distance in kilometres (km) and miles (mi); the principal sights; and, often, a brief introduction. Next comes a sentence or two on the approach roads from the departure town to bring you to the recommended starting point of the tour. This is followed by a paragraph setting the historical background. Then comes the recommended tour. The places I reckon to be outstanding are in CAPITALS. Many other places are mentioned, and you may think the capitals should have been awarded elsewhere. The names are mostly in French because signs in France tend to be in French.

The destinations are described under the departure towns which seem most convenient. But a few of the destinations can be reached from more than one of the ten departure points. For example, Mont-St-Michel, an easy day-trip from St Malo, can also be visited from Caen. Its description comes under St Malo but under Caen you will find it listed, with the distance stated and a cross-reference (*) to St Malo. Cross-reference asterisks (*) are occasionally found in a text entry: if you then turn to the main entry for that place (see index) you will find something to fill out the story of the town you are in.

Square brackets ([ ]) indicate parts of a tour which can be omitted if time is short. 'S.I.' for '*Syndicat d'Initiative*' is the standard French abbreviation for a tourist information office and I have adopted it. You may also find the international symbol 'i' for information.

Opening times

National museums and art galleries in France are closed on Tuesdays and almost all public galleries are closed between 12 noon and 2 p.m. Most open at 9.30 a.m. during the summer months and 10.00 a.m. in the winter; closing times range from 5.30 to 6.30 p.m., but check at the S.I. to be sure.

French public holidays

New Year's Day; Eastern Sunday; Easter Monday; 1 May (May Day); Ascension Day (the 40th day after Easter); Whit Sunday; Whit Monday; 14 July (Bastille Day, France's national day); 15 August (the Feast of the Assumption); 1 November (All Saints' Day); 11 November (Armistice Day); Christmas Day.

Motoring documents and regulations

In addition to your driving licence and log book, you will need an international driving permit. Be sure you have full insurance cover; the Green Card, or international insurance certificate, although no longer a legal requirement, is still accepted as proof of insurance cover.

A red warning triangle and hazard lights are obligatory in case of breakdown. Driver and front seat passengers are obliged to wear seat belts while children under ten must be on the rear seat.

Speeding and drink-driving regulations are strictly enforced usually by summary on-the-spot fines. In extreme cases the vehicle may be confiscated.

Caravan owners

You will need the logbook of the caravan as well as that of

the car pulling it. Customs may require an inventory. For evidence of insurance a Green Card Endorsement will be needed. If you plan to take a boat with you, you will need a *carnet* for any craft over 5.5 metres and for any motorboat.

French Rail

Only three of the day-trips described in this book actually require the use of the train – Paris to Beaune-Dijon, Paris to Lyon, and Arles to Lyon. However, thanks to generous government subsidies, the SNCF is one of the finest rail services in Europe and is, since it is not required to operate at or even near a profit, very reasonably priced for the individual traveller. In France, as anywhere, however, it is cheaper for families to travel by car. There is a range of bargain rail passes but these will appeal only to people who are planning to spend most of their holiday travelling. For people making the occasional day-trip from a fixed base, that is, most users of this book, these passes will be of less interest. If you should want to make use of these passes, it is advisable to buy them before you leave Britain. Details are available from the French Rail office in London, address below, or from most major British Rail stations, where you can also purchase the passes. Unfortunately, there is nothing to match the handsome discounts on day travel available with a British Rail day return.

Useful addresses

French National Tourist Office
178 Piccadilly
London W1V 0AL
Telephone: 01-491 7622

Brittany Ferries
Brittany Centre
Wharf Road
Portsmouth
Telephone 0705 827701

Sealink Ferries
Sealink Travel Centre
Victoria Station
London SW1
Telephone: 01-834 8122
24-hour recorded information:
01-834 4142

French Railways
179 Piccadilly
London Q1V 0AL
Telephone: 01-409 1224

Sally Line
81 Piccadilly
London W1
Telephone: 01-409 2240

Townsend Thoresen
127 Regent Street
London W1
Telephone: 01-734 4431

Architectural and artistic terms

Writers of guide books are prone to use art-historical terms which have a precise meaning for the specialist but are not always familiar to laymen. This short guide provides concise definitions for terms used in the pages that follow.

altarpiece Although any work of art set behind a church altar may be called an altarpiece, the word tends to be reserved for a large work consisting of a number of panel paintings, held in wooden frames. These may be ornately carved and hinged so as to fold in on themselves. See below under *triptych* and *polyptych*. A sculptured altarpiece is called a reredos.

ambulatory (from the Latin *ambulare*, to walk) In large churches, a processional aisle running behind the high altar.

apse A sanctuary, usually semi-circular but sometimes polygonal in shape, behind the high altar of a church. A large church may have a number of small chapels radiating off the ambulatory: these are known as 'apsidal chapels'.

bailey An area of a castle enclosed by a curtain wall but outside the central keep.

baroque The term for the increasingly ornate and dramatic style in European art and architecture from about 1600 to 1750. The baroque style reached its zenith in France from abut the 1660s to the early 1700s.

chancel The part of a church which includes the high altar and the choir, sometimes divided from the nave by a screen and formerly reserved for the clergy conducting the service.

chapter house The room or building of a great church where the meetings of the governing body of 'chapter' were held.

chartreuse French for charterhouse, a Carthusian monastery.

clerestory The range of windows (literally, 'clearstorey') above the triforium of a church nave.

coffered ceiling One which is deeply panelled.

corbel One which is deeply panelled.

corbel A block of stone projecting from a wall to serve as a bracket or support.

crocket A carved stone ornament, often in the shape of an upturned leaf.

curtain wall A stretch of wall in a castle between towers or bastions which is not structural but merely defensive.

drapery The representation in painting or sculpture of the folds of a garment. Artists often used this semi-abstract area of a work for highly expressive patterns of line.

flamboyant The term used for a style prevalent in French architecture in the fourteenth and fifteenth centuries. Coined from *flamber*, to flame, because of the flame-like ornaments on the window tracery.

Gothic The term, derived from the barbarian Goths, was coined in the seventeenth century as a derisive description for the architectural style from the twelfth to the fifteenth centuries. The hallmarks were the pointed arch, elaborate vaulting and an increasing use of glass and intricate window tracery. The soaring spires and flying buttresses were very different from the heavier Romanesque style.

hôtel Until about 1700 the word meant not a public hostel but the great town house of an aristocrat or wealthy merchant.

Lady chapel A chapel within a large church or a cathedral dedicated to Our Lady, the Blessed Virgin Mary.

machicolation   In castle architecture, a stone gallery projecting from a wall from which missiles could be hurled down at attackers.

misericord   A tip-up seat in a church choir with a rest to support the singers during long periods of standing during the service. The underside was often embellished with carvings, usually of everyday life or popular sayings.

needlepoint lace   A technique of lace-making in which decorative motifs are worked with needle and thread over a design drawn on paper.

Norman   While in England this is a common term for the Romanesque style of architecture prevalent after the Norman conquest, in this book it is used simply as an adjective meaning from or relating to Normandy.

polyptych   A large painting, usually a church altarpiece, comprising three or more hinged panels which can be folded in on themselves. The commonest form is the triptych.

Renaissance   Though the precise meaning of the term is much debated it broadly describes a movement in European learning and the arts beginning in Italy in about the year 1400 and spreading gradually throughout the continent. In architecture it meant the abandonment of the soaring, pointed arches and spires of the Gothic style in favour of the columns and rectangular forms of classical architecture. The French Renaissance style in architecture did not really get under way until the early 1500s.

Rococo   A light, elegant style of interior decoration, art and architecture which originated in France in the early 1700s in reaction to the heavy baroque Louis XIV style.

Romanesque   The style of European architecture from the mid-tenth to the mid-twelfth centuries. It was characterized by the round arch, massive pillars, thick walls, small windows and tunnel vaults. From about the 1160s it gave place to the lighter, soaring style of Gothic.

rood screen   A chancel screen on which is mounted a carved crucifix, in Old English the holy 'rood'.

rose window   In Gothic architecture a large round window, usually at the W. end of a church though sometimes in the end walls of the transept. The stone tracery radiates like spokes or, in later examples, like the veins of a leaf.

tapestry   A textile hanging with a design woven into it by coloured weft threads of varied length across a fixed warp. The word is sometimes loosely used of designs embroidered on linen or similar backing, as in the Bayeux 'tapestry'.

transept   In a cruciform church the part of the structure which forms the crosspiece. In fact, it is usually considered as two structures, the N. and the S. transept.

triforium   A blind arcade (i.e. without windows) running above the principal arches of the nave of a Gothic church.

triptych   A large painting, usually a church altarpiece, consisting of three framed panels hinged so that the outer two can be folded in on the central one. The backs of these outer panels are sometimes painted with non-devotional themes which are on show when the sacred picture is closed.

Trips from the
CHANNEL PORTS

CALAIS

Amiens	(Boulogne)	125 km (78 mi)
	(Calais)	159 km (99 mi)
Arras	(Boulogne)	116 km (72½ mi)
	(Calais)	112 km (70 mi)
Bruges	(Boulogne)	144 km (90 mi)
	(Calais)	111 km (70 mi)
Ghent	(Boulogne)	190 km (119 mi)
	(Calais)	156 km (97 mi)
Le Touquet	(Boulogne)	32 km (20 mi)
	(Calais)	66 km (41 mi)

CALAIS and ST OMER

There is more to Calais than its supermarkets, and an enjoyable morning or afternoon can be had exploring the town and neighbouring St Omer, where the restaurant of the commercial hotel is well patronized by the locals.

Captured by King Edward III after his victory at Crécy in 1346, Calais remained in English hands until its recovery by a French force in 1558 in the reign of Queen Mary I. The World Wars destroyed most of the old town, though the thirteenth-century watch tower, the Tour du Guet, still rises over the Place d'Armes. Outside the Hôtel de Ville Rodin's statuary group 'The Burghers of Calais' (1895) commemorates the famous events of the town's capitulation to Edward III in 1347, following months under siege. Claiming to be hereditary king of France, he considered the townsmen traitors; by medieval laws of war they could expect no mercy. Six leading citizens, in rags and with nooses round their necks, were chosen by lot to dissuade Edward from vengeance. After intercession from his beloved Queen Philippa, Edward spared their lives. But the citizens were driven out as refugees and the place settled by English families and English sympathizers. Rodin portrayed the burghers as bedraggled figures displaying emotions from resigned defiance to apprehension and despair. Expecting a conventional monument of idealized heroes, the nineteenth-century city fathers were dismayed to receive, instead, a masterpiece.

Echoes of the English period can be seen in the style of the fourteenth/fifteenth-century brick-built church of Nôtre Dame. The connection continued long after the French re-conquest. Calais's art gallery (Parc Richelieu) contains a fine collection of water colours by Richard Parkes Bonington (1800-28), who lived and worked here. A friend of Delacroix, Bonington was much admired in France. In the town's cemetery lies Nelson's mistress Lady Hamilton. The hero of Trafalgar left his beloved Emma as a 'bequest to the nation' in his will: the nation left her to end her days in humiliating poverty in a French sea port (her house stood at 27 R. Française).

Calais's traditional industries of fishing and lace-making are recalled in the restored fishermen's quarter of Le Courgain opposite the hoverport and in the lace collection in the Museum.

ST OMER

Take the N.43 from Calais: distance 40 km (25 mi)

For much of its history St Omer was a frontier town — remains of the seventeenth-century ramparts designed by Vauban can be seen in the Public Gardens. During World War I it was a British military HQ and the Royal Flying Corps had a base here. The town suffered heavy bombing during World War II. The medieval church of Nôtre Dame is notable for its fine tower and Last Judgement sculptures over the S. portal. Inside, notice the two Flamboyant-style rose windows, the panelling in the choir and the carved tombs and grilles dating from the Renaissance. The museum (14 R. Carnot) has collections of paintings, ivories, Delftware, arms and clay pipes. From 1592 to 1762 St Omer was home to an English Catholic boys' college, the origin of Stonyhurst School in Lancashire. The commercial hotel with its restaurant is in the main square.

BOULOGNE

For ferryloads of English shoppers, Boulogne is the ideal day-trip destination; it is well worth taking time to explore it. Make straight for the old town (Haute Ville) within its intact circuit of thirteenth/seventeenth-century ramparts at the top of the town (best approached by the R. de la Lampe and the Grand Rue).

The invasion fleet of the Emperor Claudius sailed from Boulogne for Britain in AD 43. During the Middle Ages the independent counts of Boulogne enjoyed occasional prominence until their territory was absorbed into France in the 1470s. Briefly conquered by Henry VIII, the town renewed its English connections in the eighteenth century when it became a favourite retirement resort for a sizeable expatriate community. Richard Martin (d. 1834), founder of the RSPCA, is buried here. The port was the principal disembarkation point for British troops during World War I and suffered heavy bombardment. Most of the remaining old town was destroyed in World War II.

You will enter the old town through an impressive fortified gateway leading to the Place Godfrey de Bouillon, named after one of the leaders of the First Crusade. One side is occupied by the elegant eighteenth-century Hôtel de Ville, a red-brick structure embellished with white stone facings and prettily proportioned dormer windows. Across the square is the thirteenth-century keep of the old castle, long used as the town belfry. There is a popular and moderately priced restaurant on the square.

The mid-nineteenth-century cathedral church replaces an earlier one which housed an ancient wooden statue of the Virgin Mary. Tradition had it that this had drifted into Boulogne harbour in a mysterious unmanned boat at some time during the seventh century. Cathedral and relic were destroyed during the Revolution. An 1875 copy of the statue remains the focus of a cult celebrated on the second Sunday after 15 August. On a fine day, a walk round the ramparts of the old town is to be recommended. There is a morning market in the Place Dalton, overlooked by the Church of St Nicholas, and good shopping: do not miss Philippe Olivier's Fromagerie at 45 R. Thiers, a mysterious corridor of a shop stacked from floor to ceiling with every conceivable variety of cheese. Boulogne is friendly to English tourists but remains proud of its association with Napoleon: it was here that he assembled the grand army and fleet of transports for his planned invasion of England.

DUNKIRK (DUNKERQUE)

The name, Flemish for 'the church on the dunes', recalls the fact that in the Middle Ages the region was part of the County of Flanders. The motorist will see many other Flemish-looking placenames on road signs approaching the Belgian frontier. The French kings claimed suzerainty over the counts and in 1658 Louis XIV ceded the town to England for Cromwell's help at the Battle of the Dunes. In 1662, the ever-improvident Charles II sold it back to France. In World War II some 350,000 men of the British and French armies were lifted from the beaches here under intense bombardment from the German airforce, and much of the town was destroyed. It suffered again during the closing months of the war as German forces held out against the Allied advance. There is a war museum in the Hôtel de Ville.

AMIENS

Route (Calais): N.1
Distance: 159 km (99 mi)
Cathedral; old quarter of St Leu; Picardy museum.

Amiens, the birthplace of Choderlos de Laclos, author of *Les Liaisons dangereuses* (1782) and of Jules Verne, makes a good destination for a day-trip. Entering along the N.1 you pass the remains of the old citadel; from here the R. St Leu leads to the cathedral (a 10-minute walk from the Gare du Nord).

Centre of the Celtic Ambiani, it was converted by St Firmin the Martyr in the fourth century, depicted over the left porch of the Cathedral's W. front. In the later Middle Ages Picardy, of which Amiens was the capital, fell to the dukes of Burgundy and then to the Spanish Habsburgs, being incorporated into France in the 1590s. The old brick-built town was severely damaged in World War I and virtually destroyed in World War II.

The survival of the CATHEDRAL of Nôtre Dame verges on the miraculous. 'One of the supreme creations of Gothic architecture' according to John Ruskin, Nôtre Dame replaced an earlier church burnt out in 1218. The nave and the W. front with its elaborate sculptural decorations were completed within 20 years. (The side chapels, transepts and upper stages of the W. towers were added over the next 200 years.) The W. front has a main central portal flanked by two smaller ones, all deeply recessed. Surmounting the central arch stands the figure of St Michael. Above the portals runs a pillared gallery and above this a band of arcading with statues of biblical kings in the niches. The great rose window between the towers is an early example of Flamboyant Gothic. The sculptures of the main door depict the Last Judgement, with Christ on the central pier and saints and angels in the vaulted arch of the porch. The right-hand porch shows the Virgin trampling down a monster. A fine St Christopher and other sculptures adorn the S. façade. Within, the glorious nave, 140 m (460 ft) long and 42 m (138 ft) high, has 126 columns rising to half its height. Notice the thirteenth-century bronze effigies in the third bay of the nave and the groin vaulting and rose windows in the transepts.

The S. transept has marble reliefs of the life of the Virgin; in the N. transept are the font from the twelfth-century church and a nineteenth-century reliquary containing the reputed head of John the Baptist, looted from Constantinople in 1204. The 110 stalls of the sixteenth-century choir feature some 3,500 figures of biblical scenes and of trades and crafts.

The restored OLD QUARTER OF ST LEU, N. of the Cathedral, retains something of the flavour of the old town in its narrow streets. To the E. of the city centre, on the N. bank of the River Somme, lies the chequerboard of canals and market gardens known as Les Hortillonages. S. of the cathedral stands the nineteenth-century Palais de Justice, with its gardens and the fifteenth-century brick and stone Logis du Roi. The MUSÉE DE PICARDIE (off the Place de la République) contains archaeological and medieval collections on the ground floor and picture galleries above. These include Chardin still-lifes, a pastel self-portrait by Maurice Quentin de la Tour, a Frans Hals and Italian pictures by, for example, Guardi and Tiepolo, as well as eighteenth-century French masterpieces. Memorabilia of Jules Verne are in the handsome seventeenth-century Hôtel des Berny, R. Victor Hugo.

ARRAS

Route (Calais): N.43 then A.26
Distance: 112 km (70 mi)
A specialist trip for enthusiasts of military history, for whom some indication of the principal sites of interest is given here. Further details of war cemeteries etc. are available from specialist publications or the local S.I.

The A.1 from Calais brings you in along the Boulevard Faidherbe to the railway station and the S.I. If your chief objective is the World War battlefields, you will find documentation here. Virtually destroyed in the two great wars of this century, the town today represents a triumph of restoration and rebuilding. The GRANDE PLACE is in seventeenth-century Flemish style while the PETITE PLACE has the restored early-1500s Hôtel de Ville with its restored Gothic belfry.

For centuries Arras was a frontier town between the lands of the Holy Roman Empire and those of the French kings. From *c*. 1500 to *c*. 1650 it was part of the Habsburg empire before being incorporated into France. It was long famous for the manufacture of wall tapestries.

During World War I Arras was close behind the Western Front. A drive along the N.39 to Cambrai, 36 km (23 mi) distant, takes you through many historic scenes of action, notably Observation Ridge, The Harp and Telegraph Hill. Marquion, the half-way point between Arras and Cambrai, was the scene of a famous Canadian victory in September 1918. S. of Arras lay the famous stretch of German fieldworks known as the Hindenburg or 'Siegfried' Line, and it was on the rolling country between Arras and Cambrai that the British launched the first tank attacks in the history of warfare.

BRUGES (BRUGGE)

Route (Calais): N.1.E.40 to Veurne, Belgium, then E.5 and
                        autoroute
Distance: 111 km (70 mi)
Grotmarkt, Market Hall and Belfry; Stadhuis (town hall);
'Gothic Hall'; Oude Griffie museum; Begijnhof convent;
Onze Lieve Vrouw church with Michelangelo statue; Sint
Jans Hospital and Memling Museum; Sint Salvatorkathedral.

It may seem surprising to have two Belgian towns in a book
about days out in France; however, Bruges and *Ghent are
among Europe's most beautiful and interesting cities and
both are a reasonable distance for a day-trip from Calais or
Dunkirk.

The chief central sites of Bruges are within easy walking
distance, but there are various additional places of interest
and it is worth skirting the city before heading for the centre.

After leaving the motorway, follow the signs for the centre
of town, the railway underpass, but turn right at the major
roundabout. Follow the ring road for about ½ km (¼ mi), at
which point it swings left and skirts the outer canal of the
city, offering fine views – notably the Gentpoort. Cross over
at the next bridge, turn right and keep straight on along
Kruisvest, with the old St Janshuismoelen windmill on your
right. On the next corner (left) stands the fifteenth-century
Guildhouse of the Archers of St Sebastian; the Queen and
Prince Philip are honorary members of the guild, and the
building contains some fine paintings, gold and silverwork.
Continue to a T-junction on a canal; round to the left is the
DE POTTERIE hospice. Its old gables make a fine show and
within there are magnificent tapestries, paintings and draw-
ings attributed to Jan van Eyck. Follow the Potteriesreie
(skirting the Reie waterway) for the centre. Carmerstraat,
fourth left, leads via Balstraat to the KANT CENTRUM
(LACE CENTRE), where there are afternoon demonstrations
of lace-making, and the Museum voor Volkskunde (Folklore
Museum). Take the fourth right (Genthof) to the Van Eyck
Plein/Jan van Eyck Plaats, where the medieval POORTERS
LOGE, once the lodge of the White Bear society, has a
famous fifteenth-century statue of a white bear with the city's
coat-of-arms between its paws. Follow Academiestraat to

Vlamingstraat (left) for the GROTMARKT, or central marketplace.

Surrounded by fine town-house façades of many centuries,
the square, dominated by its famous medieval BELFRY (83
m, 272 ft), recalls the heroic days of Bruges' prosperity and
independence. In the Middle Ages Flanders was the industrial
and financial heartland of northern Europe; Bruges and
*Ghent led the cities' opposition to the local counts, who
were often allies of the French king. The nineteenth-century
monument in the Grotmarkt records the leaders of the Bruges
Matins rising against the French in 1302, followed by the
victorious Battle of the Spurs, named from the immense
plunder taken from the French knights. The belfries of
Flanders punctuated the landscape and the music of their
bells (once used to rally the citizens to arms) provides regular
public concerts. Climbing to the Belfry, more than 4,350
steps, past the carillon drum mechanism, brings the reward of
a panoramic view over miles of the surrounding countryside.
The tower rises from the old market hall (Tourist Information) with a fine courtyard.

Leave the square by Breidelstraat, skirting the Post Office
for the Burg square with the 1660s Landshuis on your left,
and opposite across the square the Basilica of the Holy Blood,
the Stadhuis (Town Hall) and the Gerechtshof (Law Courts).
The BASILICA has a twelfth-century Lower Chapel dedicated to St Basil and an Upper Chapel (fifteenth and sixteenth
centuries) with colourful mosaics and an early-1600s silver
reliquary that holds the phial allegedly containing drops of
the blood of Christ (presented to a twelfth-century count of
Flanders by the Patriarch of Jerusalem, while on crusade).
The Museum of the Holy Blood contains a gold- and
silver-jewelled reliquary (1610s) and Van Dyck's *Adoration
of the Magi*. The remarkable STADHUIS, completed in the
early 1400s (the oldest surviving in Belgium), is adorned with
niches housing statues of the medieval counts and countesses
of Flanders (nineteenth-century replacement of originals destroyed by the French Revolutionary army). Inside, the
superb timbered roof of the GOTHIC HALL really should be
seen. Left of the Stadhuis is the beautiful mid-sixteenth-
century official residence called the OUDE GRIFFIE; beyond
lies the Gerechtshof. Now a museum, it has a handsome
black marble Renaissance chimneypiece enriched with oak

carvings, dating from the early 1500s, of Habsburg and Spanish rulers.

The alley under the Oude Griffie leads over the main canal to the old Fish Market. Turn to admire the attractive townscape of the old buildings lining the canal. There is a good fish restaurant in the old Fish Market, but do not miss the charming little Huidvetters Plaats, or 'Tanners' Square', with its lamp standards, cosy houses and restaurants. Now a quiet little pedestrian precinct, in its heyday it must have been one of the foulest areas of old Bruges with the waste from the tanneries draining into the canal.

Now turn right along the canal with the fine old houses on the opposite bank and glimpses of old arcaded and galleried streets on your left. Notice the College of Europe and the Arentshuis Museum, containing pictures of old Bruges and works by the British artist Frank Brangwyn (d. 1956), who was born in Bruges. Next visit the GROENINGEN MUSEUM, which has one of the world's finest collections of Flemish fifteenth-century paintings, housed in a fine new building in the old courtyard.

Leaving the museum, you find yourself crossing a canal with the lofty tower of the church of Onze Lieve Vrouw (Our Lady) ahead. Left, a delightful short walk brings you to a charming picturesque Benedictine nunnery, the medieval Begijnhof and beyond this the quiet lakeside gardens of the Minnewater. From here you have one of Europe's loveliest townscape views.

Now return to the magnificent church of ONZE LIEVE VROUW. The body of the church dates from the early 1200s, the aisles from the fourteenth and fifteenth centuries. There are fine paintings and carvings by sixteenth- and seventeenth-century Flemish masters, but the church's chief treasure is the white marble 'Virgin and Child' by Michelangelo in the chapel at the E. end of the S. aisle (turn right on entering the church). In the choir (with the armorial bearings of the Knights of the Golden Fleece painted above the eighteenth-century stalls) are the magnificent heraldic mausoleums of Duke Charles the Bold of Burgundy (d. 1477) and his daughter Mary (d. 1482), whose marriage brought the Low Countries to the Habsburg family. Hers, erected about 1500, is generally reckoned the finer.

Near the church stands the SINT JANS Hospital with its

magnificent Great Hall (*c.* 1300). It holds a fascinating collection of medical items and, in the former chapel, the MEMLING MUSEUM in which Hans Memling's *Mystic Marriage of St Catherine* (1479) triptych has pride of place. The central panel depicts the Virgin enthroned with the Child on her lap; to the left a kneeling St Catherine receives from the Infant Jesus the ring symbolizing the mystic marriage of the saintly Virgin to the Godhead. St John the Baptist and St John the Evangelist flank the throne and their stories are told on the outer panels.

Now follow the Heiligegeestraat to the SINT SALVATOR-KATHEDRAAL (St Saviour's). The thirteenth-century church achieved cathedral status only in 1834, the French having destroyed the old cathedral in 1799 (Napoleon abolished the bishopric). The 1430s choir stalls were commissioned to mark the founding of Duke Philip the Good of Burgundy's founding of the chivalric order of the Golden Fleece. The armorial blazons above them date from 1478, when the 13th Chapter of the Order convened to deliberate the fate of the Burgundian lands following the death of Duke Charles the Bold at the Battle of Nancy the previous year. The five apsidal chapels giving off the ambulatory contain two fine fifteenth-century altarpieces and a monumental brass from the early 1550s. The adjacent Cathedral Museum was built early in this century.

Returning to the Grotmarkt along Oudeburg enjoy the fine sixteenth- and seventeenth-century house façades and stop off in Simon Stevinplaats (morning FLOWER MARKET), commemorative of the late sixteenth-century Flemish mathematician who pioneered Europe's adoption of the decimal system.

GHENT (GENT)

**Route (Calais): N.1.E.40 to Veurne, Belgium, then E.5 and
            autoroute**
Distance: 156 km (97 mi)
*Sint Baafskathedral with Van Eyck's Adoration of the Lamb;
Gerard Duivelsteen, thirteenth-century tower house; Cloth
Hall; 'S Gravensteen castle; Klein Begijnhof convent;
medieval and Renaissance townscapes and mansions.*

Ghent's medieval prosperity, built on the cloth industry,
fuelled recurring conflicts with the counts of Flanders, whose
chief castle was here. In 1302 Ghent and Bruges defeated a
French army supporting the count at the 'Battle of the Spurs';
in the 1340s, under Jacob van Artevelde (d. 1345), Ghent
allied with Edward III of England against France (John of
Gaunt was born here). In the 1380s defeat by the French and
a dynastic marriage brought Flanders to the French duke
Philip the Bold of Burgundy. The fifteenth-century Burgundian Low Countries enjoyed a golden age. Jan van Eyck was
just one of many great painters, though Duke Philip the Good
drastically curtailed Ghent's liberties. The death of his son,
Charles the Bold (1477), ended the Burgundian period and
Charles's heiress, Duchess Mary, had to restore lost liberties
in the Great Privilege of Ghent. Her marriage brought the
Low Countries under the authority of the Austrian Habsburg
rulers. Emperor Charles V was born in Ghent (1500) and

punished the city ruthlessly for a rising in 1535. Fifty years later the Low Countries became part of the Spanish empire. Ghent's modern prosperity dates from the introduction of English-style textile mills in the early 1800s and the opening of the Terneuzen ship canal in the 1820s. The foundation of Belgium in 1830 prepared the way for a resurgence of Flemish nationalism, of which Ghent was an important centre. Today, rich in historic buildings, a major centre of the horticultural industry and with a busy port, it ranks with Europe's greatest cities. Its international trade fair is held in September; in August at nearby Lochristi there is an annual begonia festival; and the Floriales flower festival is held every five years.

SINT BAAFSKATHEDRAL (St Bavon's), originally St John's, was rededicated when the chapter of St Baaf's Abbey (demolished by Emperor Charles V in the 1540s) moved here. The large and well proportioned interior is full of paintings, sculptures, tombs and elaborate pieces of church furniture. But the glory of Ghent is van Eyck's *ADORATION OF THE MYSTIC LAMB* (in the sixth chapel off the ambulatory round the thirteenth-century choir). An inscription states that it was begun by Hubert van Eyck and completed by Jan van Eyck (his brother) in 1432. Hubert's contribution, even his very existence, has been disputed. Twelve panels, mounted on a central section and two hinged wings, extend 4.5 m (14 ft 8 in) by 3.5 m (11 ft 3 in). The work derives its name from the central lower panel. In a verdant, flowery meadow amidst groves of trees stands an altar with the sacrificial Lamb of God surrounded by angels and in front of it the fountain of life. A nimbus in the sky sends its rays down on to the landscape where groups of holy virgins, clerics and nobles approach. The wide panorama is portrayed with a jewel-like precision of detail which was the hallmark of Jan van Eyck's style (botanists have identified more than 40 plants and flower species exactly depicted). To the left, the Just Judges and Warriors of Christ troop towards the field of worship through rocky landscapes; to the right are hermits and pilgrims. Above, God the Father sits enthroned, flanked by the Virgin and St John, while the outer panels on this tier comprise monumental nudes (the first in northern art) of Adam and Eve, a choir and the famous St Caecilia (patron saint of music) seated at an organ. When closed the outer

wings reveal portraits of the donors Joos Vydt and his wife
Isabel Borluut, and the Annunciation. The masterpiece survived the Calvinist iconoclasm that swept Ghent in the 1560s
only to be looted by the French during the Revolutionary
period (it was returned in 1815). In 1934 the 'Just Judges'
panel was stolen. The 1941 copy, of outstanding quality,
includes a portrait of King Leopold III of the Belgians (Van
Eyck's original includes portraits of numerous contemporary
notabilities). Before leaving the Cathedral do not miss the
Rubens altarpiece in the tenth ambulatory chapel, with its
bearded self-portrait, or the fifteenth-century triptych by
Justus van Ghent in the N. aisle.

E. of the Cathedral the GERARD DUIVELSTEEN (Castle
of Gerard the Devil) looks out over the Scheldt. This
thirteenth-century tower house with its fine Romanesque
crypt is the last of the numerous 'great houses built in their
haughty pride by the men of Ghent' much to the annoyance
of the medieval counts.

Ahead is the fifteenth-century LAKENHALLE (Cloth
Hall); the guild chamber on the first floor has an audiovisual
presentation of Ghent's conflicts with Charles V. The
fourteenth-century BELFRY contains a famous carillon of 52
bells (seventeenth and eighteenth centuries). The Bell Roelant
(1310s) sounded the citizens' call to arms; Charles V later
ordered its removal. Atop the belfry's restored spire the
gilded copper 1370s Dragon weather vane is more than 3 m
(10 ft) long. (A short walk up Botermarkt and Borluutstraat
brings you to the Tourist Information, but return to continue
our tour from the Belfry.)

Beyond in the Burgemeester Braunplein is the Fountain of
the Kneeling Figures and the massive TRIOMFANTE BELL
(1660); off to the right notice the charming early-1500s
gabled house 'De Fonteyn'. Skirting St Nicholas's church
down Klein Turkije you come to the RODE HOED ('Red
Hat') inn, where Albrecht Dürer lodged in 1521. The tower
of SINT NIKLAASKERK (1300) was the town's first belfry
and first rallying point to arms. It looks out over the
KOORNMARKT (corn market), the historic centre of
Ghent: the medieval BORLUUT MANSION was the home of
Jan Borluut, who led the Ghent men at the Battle of the Spurs
(1302) and the storming of 'S Gravensteen in the same year.

On the St MICHELSBRUG bridge over the River Leie

(Lys) pause for one of Europe's most famous views. To the N.
lie the mansions, guild houses and warehouses of Ghent's
golden past. Along the Koornlei ('Grain Wharf'), left, notice
the gilded boat on the Huis der Onvrije Schippers (boatmen
who were not freemen of Ghent). The GRASLEI ('Herb
Wharf') is yet more splendid, its marvellous Romanesque
Spijker grain warehouse dating from the early 1200s. Across
the bridge, St Michael's church contains a *Crucifixion* by van
Dyck and next to it the 'Pand' priory has a fine Gothic library
building commissioned in the 1470s by Duke Charles the
Bold's English wife, Margaret.

Follow the Koornlei into Jan Dreydellstraat and the
museum of decorative arts (Sierkunst) at no. 7. At the
junction with Burgstraat and Gewad notice the 1500s
'Crowned Heads' House' with stepped gables and voluted
gables and portrait heads of the counts of Flanders. From the
Reckelinkestraad bridge you have an excellent view of 'S
GRAVENSTEEN, the Castle of the Counts, with its great
central keep, the counts' house with stepped gables, and the
unusual hanging turrets over the moat (notice the drain holes
from which latrines discharged). The lower levels of the keep
survive from a fortress built for defence against Norse
invaders in the ninth century; the main structure dates from
the late twelfth when Count Philip began building a new
bastion 'to humble the overbearing arrogance of the men of
Ghent'. The tour, following a numbered route, begins with
the gatehouse. Virtually a small castle in its own right, it juts
out some 20 m (60 ft) from the main walls, its entrance
defended by two machicolated towers. The upper room, with
its cross-shaped window, may have been the original chapel.
Descending to the keep's cellars, you can see the remains of
the original fortress and punishment cells or *oubliettes*, deep
pits with only trap doors for entrances. A passage along the
outer wall brings you to the counts' residence. The audience
chamber is notable for its heavy vaulting supported by two
free-standing pillars and wall corbels. The counts' court of
justice and later the Council of Flanders sat here. On the next
floor is the 'Countess's Chamber' and a terrible collection of
torture instruments. You continue through the Upper Hall to
the roof, with a dramatic view of the city. From here you
descend to the Great Hall. Here, in 1454, Duke Philip the
Good presided over the seventh chapter of the chivalric

Order of the Golden Fleece, the knights dressed 'in scarlet robes and wearing golden collars of arquebuses belching flames from which hung the insignia of the order'. You leave the castle via the subterranean vaulted crypt, ventilated by air shafts and used as stables.

From the St Veerleplein follow the Kraanlei past the folk history ('Volkskunde') museum, in a range of medieval almshouses, and some pretty carved gables at nos. 77 and 79. Over the Zuivelbrug bridge you come to Groot Kanonplein and the famous cast-iron cannon (1430) 'Dulle Griet' ('Mad Meg'). In the VRIJDAGMARKT ('Friday market') stands a nineteenth-century statue of Jacob van Artevelde (1287–1345). The market was the great assembly point of the citizens in thier struggles with the counts. Continuing along the Kammerstraat you pass the late-1400s Tanners' Guild-house (Toreken) on your right; a street opposite leads to St Jacobskirk.

At the corner of Botermarkt and Nederpolder stands the 1470s Sint JORISHOF (St George's Court), once the seat of the Crossbowmen's Guild where Duchess Mary signed the Great Privilege. Up Nederpolder are the finest of Ghent's old mansions, the Grote Moor and Zwarte Moor and the famous group of the GROTE SIKKEL (*c.* 1300), the thirteenth-century KLEINE SIKKEL and opposite this the sumptuous sixteenth/eighteenth-century Van der Meersch hotel. Turn right down the Biezerkapelstraat for the courtyard in which stands the late-medieval Achter Sikkel. Return to the Hoog-port, dominated by the magnificent Flamboyant façade of the mid-seventeenth-century STADHUIS (town hall) and so, via the Botermarkt, to the Cloth Hall and St Baafsplein.

E. of the cathedral, the Vlanderenstraat leads to Lange Violettestraat and KLEIN BEGIJNHOF ('Little Beguinage' convent founded in the thirteenth century), a charming group of seventeenth/nineteenth-century buildings surrounding a quiet enclosure.

Additional sights include the Fine Arts Museum ('Schone Konsten') near the Festpaleis, the Bijloke Museum (history of Flanders) in beautiful old abbey buildings on the Gods-huizenlaan, and the remains of St Bavon's Abbey (Abdij Sint Baaf) on the Lousbergskai (birthplace of John of Gaunt). St Peter's Abbey (seventeenth century) on the St Pietersplein houses a youth hostel.

LE TOUQUET

Route (Calais): N.1 to Boulogne, then D. 940; 66 km (41 mi)
Route (Boulogne): D.940; 32 km (20 mi)
Route (Dieppe): D.925 to Eu, then D.940; 125 km (78 mi)
Luxury resort.

With its superb beach, set in the middle of the Opal coast, Le Touquet boasts 'a touch of fashion and plenty of France'. In the high days between the Wars it was very chic and smart. Among the expatriate British community, P.G. Wodehouse had a house here until he was interned by the Germans. The pine woods behind the town are studded with luxury villas. Numerous nightclubs offer quality entertainment and there is a choice of two luxury casinos: Casino de la Plage in the R. de Paris and Casino de la Forêt (*boule*) and Place de l'Hermitage (roulette and baccarat). Both are open from 30 June to early/mid-September. Top-class restaurants offer gourmet menus; alternatively, you can eat in one of the bistro cafés. Shopping is good, and there is a locally renowned open market (Thursdays, Saturdays and Mondays, also July to mid-September). Beach facilities include a children's club, sand-yachting and a heated, open-air sea-water pool. There are two 18-hole and one 9-hole golf courses, a tennis club with its own heated swimming pool, various riding centres and fishing in the nearby Canche estuary. For details of these latter and the possibilities of a day's sailing with the Cercle Nautique enquire at the S.I.

There are numerous sporting tournaments – show-jumping, horse-racing, sand-yachting, golf and tennis in June and July, an Easter Film Festival and an International Bridge Tournament in September.

DIEPPE

Fécamp		64 km (40 mi)
Château Gaillard		101 km (63 mi)
Giverny (Vernon)		114 km (71 mi)
Rouen		61 km (38 mi)
Amiens	*Calais	102 km (64 mi)
Honfleur	*Caen	139 km (88 mi)
Le Touquet	*Calais	125 km (78 mi)

As devotees of the Newhaven ferry know, Dieppe rewards exploration. A cross-Channel service began operating between Dieppe and Brightelmstone (now Brighton) in the 1790s and in the nineteenth century, being the closest beach to Paris, Dieppe became a fashionable resort. There are lingering echoes of former stylishness in GRANDE RUE (behind the Gare Maritime), with its high-class charcuteries and 'very nice' if somewhat dowdy Salon de Thé.

A Norse settlement in the ninth century, the deep-water harbour (the name derives from Old Norse '*djupr*', 'deep') was defended in the twelfth when Henry II, King of England and Duke of Normandy, built a castle here. Later it became a base for privateers, sea rovers operating under French royal licence chiefly against the Channel ports and shipping of England. Early in the 1500s a squadron commanded by Francis I's minister Jean Ango forced the Portuguese to open the African shipping routes to French trade. Ango became royal governor of Dieppe and built himself a couple of mansions out of his plunder. One, the Manoir Ango, still stands some 8 km (5 mi) W. along the D.75 coast road. In the seventeenth century Dieppois were prominent in the settlement of Canada. In August 1942 Dieppe was the objective of the controversial Canadian Commando raid in which only 2000 men out of a force of 7000 survived a murderous German defensive barrage.

From the Grand Rue walk down to the Boulevard de Verdun, the lovely and spacious promenade giving on to a greensward and from there to the beach. The W. end is dominated by a CASTLE surmounting a hill. The central round tower dates from the fourteenth century, the rest of the structure (much restored after war damage) from the later Middle Ages. The MUSEUM is worth a visit. In the nineteenth century Dieppe was something of an artists' colony; Pissarro and Sickert both worked here and the museum has works by them as well as an important collection of prints by Georges Braque. There is a department of maritime history with some fascinating ship models and an extensive collection of carved ivories. Thanks to Ango's opening up of trade with Africa, ivory was a major import and during the seventeenth century some 300 ivory carvers worked in Dieppe.

Stroll back two blocks along the Boulevard de Verdun for the old casino. A right turn brings you to the Church of St Rémy, an unusually late (*c.* 1600) example of Norman Gothic with a fine chancel and baroque organ case. From here, via the Place du Puits, fork right from the Grande Rue to the CHURCH OF ST JACQUES, an imposing Gothic structure. The grand fourteenth-century W. door (rose window above) opens into a thirteenth-century nave; the tower dates from the 1400s and the various radiating chapels at the E. end from the 1500s. Mostly built by rich privateers, some of these have scenes recording their explorations – notice the frieze of Brazilian Indians over the sacristy door. From here it is a short step back to the old fishing port with its morning fish auctions. There is a town MARKET on Tuesdays, Thursdays and Saturdays, fishing and riding (ask at the S.I., near the Parc Jehan Ango). Take the D.75 west for the GOLF COURSE and the MUSÉE DE 19 AOÛT 1942, commemorating the Canadian Commando raid.

FÉCAMP

Route (Dieppe): D.925
Distance: 64 km (40 mi)
La Trinité Church; Benedictine distillery; Guy de Maupassant.

The D.925 brings you in along the Route de Cany to the fishing PORT. Turn left and, at the T-junction with the Quay Bérigny, left again for the Boulevard de la République and the great church of La Trinité, all that is left of the once extensive complex of abbey buildings.

There was a monastery here from the seventh century when, according to tradition, drops of Christ's blood fell to earth here. Duke Richard II of Normandy founded an abbey in the early eleventh century. For many years the richest in the duchy, it was known as 'Heaven's Gate' from the glories of its treasures. The present church of LA TRINITÉ dates from a twelfth-century rebuilding and still holds the relic of the Sacred Blood. The eighteenth-century façade is quite out of style with the great Gothic church lying behind it. Built mainly between the 1170s and 1220s, the structure is noted for the austerely magnificent nave, the thirteenth-century lantern tower and the stately proportions of the chancel. The S. transept, to the right of the eighteenth-century choir stalls, contains a beautiful fifteenth-century sculptural depiction of the Virgin (the 'Dormition'). Near the altar notice the 'Angel's footprint'. Continuing down the aisle with the chancel and its eighteenth-century high altar on your left, you come to the first ambulatory chapel, containing the tomb of a fourteenth-century abbot carved with scenes from the abbey's history. Further on you can see the white marble Renaissance tabernacle which holds the relic of the Sacred Blood. Ahead lies the Flamboyant-style Lady Chapel. The ambulatory brings you round to the N. chancel aisle with its side chapels and the N. transept, with carvings from the old rood screen and an elaborate mid-seventeenth-century clock.

From the church the R. Leroux, continued under various names down to the sea-front, leads first to the Municipal Museum (local history and other exhibits) and then on to the BENEDICTINE DISTILLERY and Museum. The famous liqueur, distilled from a closely guarded recipe combining pure spirit, extracts from some forty herbs and other ingredients, evolved in the fifteenth century from experiments in the old abbey garden for, of course, purely medicinal purposes. Bénédictine claims to be the world's oldest liqueur. No longer manufactured by monks, it still bears the legend 'DOM' (Deo Optimo Maximo – 'To God, Most Good, Most Great'). There are daily conducted tours of the distillery, while the museum holds collections of items ranging from charters to statues from the former abbey.

Though born here, Guy de Maupassant spent his infancy and childhood at Dieppe. However, he often returned to Fécamp, which provided the settings for some of his stories.

CHÂTEAU GAILLARD –
Les Andelys

Route (Dieppe): N.27/A.15 to Rouen, then follow the signs for the N.14 for Pontoise and Les Andelys; at the village of Ecouis take the D.2/D.1
Distance: 101 km (63 mi) (For alternative route *Giverny)
One of Normandy's most historic sites.

The twin townships of Grand and Petit Andely stand at a break in sweeping white cliffs on a bend in the River Seine. Above sit the menacing ruins of Richard of England's Château Gaillard (1196-9).

The D.1 brings you to a T-junction with the Ave de la République in the centre of town. Turn left for the S.I. and the Church of Nôtre Dame (good sixteenth-century glass, S. aisle). The R. Louis-Pasteur continues on the D.1 route to the ascent for the castle. Turn right at the crossroads out of town. A gradient of 1:6 leads to the car park with its splendid VIEW of the Seine and the Island of Andely (see map, page 36).

The CASTLE was built by King Richard I, the Lionheart, after his return from the Crusades (1194). It was part of a strategy to fortify his lands in France against encroachments made by the French king, Philip II Augustus. Gaillard, his 'Saucy Castle', defended the Seine crossing on the Norman frontier. It stands on a rocky plateau, the ground plunging away sharply on almost every side. There is a forward or

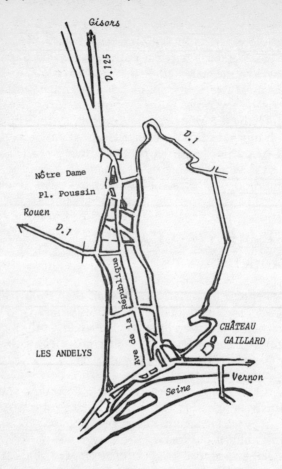

Outer Bailey, a Middle Bailey, divided from it by a deep moat, and an Inner Bailey with a massive donjon or Keep. The lie of the land forced attackers to take each in turn: you will follow the same route.

The path from the car park leads to the gate of the Outer Bailey, of which a section of wall and the principal forward tower survive. Crossing the ruins of the Middle Bailey you come to the inner ring of fortifications with the governor's lodging and the dramatic keep, which still rises to some two-thirds of its original height. The rounded contours of the tower reflect developments in twelfth-century military architecture to help withstand improved stone-throwing machines, called *trebuchets*. The unusual inverted buttresses carried machicolations – stone fighting galleries from which defenders could fire down on attackers. Such details were more or less standard. It is the choice of site and the brilliant exploitation of the natural defensive possibilities that confirm Richard I as not only the finest soldier but also the leading military architect of his age. Additional defence works were provided by the fortified town of Andely, piles driven into the river to hamper water-borne attack, and a tower on Andely Island. Beneath the castle, undercrofts were hewn from the rock to hold stores and garrison quarters.

Richard died in 1199, to be succeeded by his brother John. In August 1203 Philip of France began the siege of Château Gaillard, one of the key episodes in medieval history. The town and river works had to be yielded after a month because of the shortage of defenders – 1500 townspeople fled for protection to the castle. The French now girdled the whole site with a double trench and walls. They taunted the defenders, 'fledglings in a crowded eyrie who will have to fly when spring arrives'. But the 300-strong garrison was well provisioned and had fresh water from the well in the middle bailey. In November Castellan Roger de Lacy drove 500 non-combattant townsfolk out through the lines. A few days later 500 more followed but a third group were refused passage by the French. For three months they cowered under the flying missiles, scratching for roots in the moat and, it is said, resorting to cannibalism. The main assault began in February. The Outer Bailey was battered into submission. The attackers now faced the ditch before the Middle Bailey. Under cover of night a soldier (Peter Snubnose, we are told) led a storming party up through latrine drains to an un-defended window in new apartments built against the outer wall (Richard would never have made such an unmilitary design). The defenders set fire to the wooden structure but the fire got out of control and they were forced to retreat to the Inner Bailey. In the third week of March 1204, after a seven-month siege and reduced to just 156 combattants, the garrison were granted terms. They had refused to surrender, expecting a relieving force from England. King John's failure to raise the siege lost him the Saucy Castle and with it the Duchy of Normandy.

From the car park the one-way road descends via the R. Richard Coeur du Lion into Petit Andely.

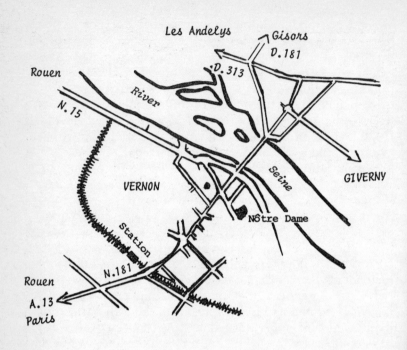

GIVERNY (Vernon)

**Route (Dieppe): N.27/A.15 to Rouen, then N.15 Paris road
to Vernon, signpost to Giverny**
Distance: 114 km (71 mi)
House and gardens of Claude Monet.

The Monet house and garden at Giverny is a place of
pilgrimage for art-lovers and a delightful visit for all garden
enthusiasts. By car it combines well with a visit to *Les
Andelys and Château Gaillard, but make an early start both
to beat the rush-hour traffic at Rouen (the most direct route
lies through the city) and the worst of the tourist coaches at
Giverny. The house opens at 10 a.m. It is only 4 km (2½ mi)
from Vernon but unless you reach Vernon well before 10
drive straight to Giverny.

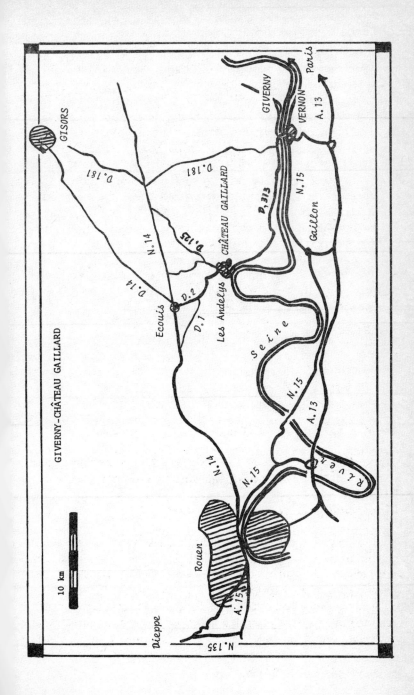

GIVERNY-CHÂTEAU GAILLARD

Claude Monet (1840-1926) settled in the quiet little village of Giverny in 1883. In the public mind he was associated with the group of young artists who rejected the polished style of the official academy and had been derisively dubbed 'Impressionists' by the critics; indeed, it was Monet's painting *Impression, Sunrise*, exhibited in 1874, which had earned them their nickname. His first wife's death five years later and a brief estrangement from the group led him to seek retreat at Giverny. In 1890 he bought the large and charmingly unpretentious house which became the family home. Here his beloved gardens absorbed more and more of his attention: the Clos Normand in front of the house and the beautiful water garden which he created across the road by diverting the nearby stream. At the age of 70 he embarked on a large-scale series of paintings inspired by the garden's water lilies. These immense and tranquil works marked a new departure which would lead him to the frontiers of his art and beyond into the realm of abstractionism. In the mid-1910s he built the extensive 'water lily studio' to work on the great scheme conceived in his 'open air studio', the garden itself. In 1918, urged by Prime Minister Clemenceau, the painter decided to donate a series of water-lily canvases to the nation to mark the ending of the Great War. The project was delayed when Monet had to undergo an operation for cataract (he died blind), but the great monument to peace was signed over for display in the Orangerie at the Tuileries in Paris in 1922.

After Monet's death the property at Giverny gradually deteriorated. In 1966 it passed by the will of his son to the Institut Français. It was opened to the public in 1980 after extensive restoration work largely financed by American donors. Today, despite us tourists, the house and gardens, once again rich in flowers and with the Japanese bridge that features in so many of his paintings renewed, offer an idea of Monet's closed and private world of beauty and contemplation.

Returning to VERNON, park near the Tour des Archives, to your right across the bridge. The little town is as old as Normandy itself, having been founded in the ninth century by Rollo, the first duke. Standing on the Seine close to the Norman border with the French kings' territories, it was a frontier fortress. The Tour des Archives was the keep of a castle built in the 1120s by Henry I, ruler of Normandy as well as king of England. Most of old Vernon was destroyed during World War II, but a short walk from the tower a group of attractive old half-timbered houses stands near the Church of Nôtre Dame. The handsome W. front, rose window and nave all date from the fifteenth century while the massive Romanesque arches of the chancel are from the original twelfth-century structure. There are some fine sixteenth-century tapestries.

For Les Andelys, about 25 km (15 mi) distant, recross the bridge and turn left, passing the Château des Tourelles, for the D.313.

ROUEN

Route (Dieppe): N.27, 4 km (2½ mi) after le Boulay N. 315 for junction with autoroute A.15; distance: 61 km (38 mi)
Route (Paris): A.13, N.138; distance: 140 km (88 mi)
Cathedral; Church of St Joan of Arc; St Maclou; Grand Horloge; Museum; antique shops; fish restaurants; Rouen Corniche.

The A.15 brings you in along the N. bank of the Seine, the N.138 over the Pont Boïeldieu (turn right). Continue along the quayside of France's fourth largest port, passing the Île Lacroix on your right, up the Ave Aristide Briand for the R. Henri Rivière and the Corniche with its dramatic PANORAMA of the city. (You may prefer to head straight for the Cathedral square, with the S.I., along the R. Grand Pont, opposite Pont Boïeldieu.) If you arrive by train, take the bus for the Cathedral.

The ancient settlement here became the Roman town of Rotomagus. Seat of an archbishopric from the fifth century, it was taken by the Norse invaders in the ninth century.

Rollo, Normandy's first duke, was born here and it became capital of the new duchy in 911. Between 1418 and 1449 it was capital of English Normandy and it was here on 21 February 1431 that the trial of Joan of Arc opened. Captured by England's ally the Duke of Burgundy and handed over in exchange for 10,000 gold pieces, she was tried as a heretic under Bishop Cauchon of Paris and burnt at the stake on 30 May. Another church court under French royal patronage rehabilitated her in 1456. In the nineteenth century her cult began to grow and in 1920 she was canonized and declared patron saint of France. The sixteenth century was a golden age and in the eighteenth the city flourished thanks to its textile industry. Most of the old city was destroyed in World War II but thanks to fine restoration many of the old buildings seem as fine today as when first built.

The CATHEDRAL, among the most beautiful in France, was begun about 1200 after fire destroyed an earlier church. The great W. front, subject of a famous series of paintings by Claude Monet, has carvings of Christ in Glory and the Martyrdom of St Stephen (right portal); the feast of Herod and the Martyrdom of St John the Baptist (left portal) and a Tree of Jesse. The twelfth-century Romanesque N. tower survives from the earlier church; the S. Butter Tower (*c.* 1500, supposedly financed by profits from indulgences sold to pardon the eating of butter during Lent) holds a 56-bell carillon. Up the R. St Romain to the left there is a good view of the thirteenth-century central tower supporting the nineteenth-century cast-iron spire. Here you can also see the Booksellers' Court, formerly a pitch for bookstalls, with Flamboyant gateway and late thirteenth-century carved portals. It is matched by the Calende Portal in the S. transept. The majestic nave with its 20 clustered columns and pointed arches and the soaring arches of the lantern tower, together with the glass in the lower windows of the chancel, are among the finest achievements of thirteenth-century Gothic. Notice the carving on the 1460s choir stalls and, in the N. transept, the Booksellers' Staircase and the fourteenth-century glass of the rose window.

Take the guided tour of the eleventh-century crypt and ambulatory chapels for the tomb of Richard the Lionheart, King of England and Duke of Normandy, and some beautiful stained glass and other tomb effigies. The fourteenth-century

Lady Chapel also has good stained glass and some fine fifteenth- and sixteenth-century tombs.

Now follow the R. St Romain between old houses and courtyards and, on your right, the looming walls of the fifteenth-century archiepiscopal palace where Joan's trial was held. Across the R. de la République lies the CHURCH OF ST MACLOU (1430s-1510s) in the Place Barthélemy, flanked by lofty half-timbered mansions with quality antique shops. St Maclou is a perfect example of the late Flamboyant style of French Gothic (nineteenth-century spire). A dramatic five-part porch projects from the façade, with delightful bronze animal heads and French Renaissance reliefs. Inside there is a sensational sixteenth-century organ loft and stone spiral staircase, and a majestic interior. The R. Martainville, past the N. side of the church and a pretty Renaissance fountain, leads to the AÎTRE ST MACLOU, a cloistered courtyard, formerly the plague cemetery. The galleries, now occupied by art studios, and window frames are carved with skulls, bones and sextons' shovels and other ghoulish mementos of death. [From here the energetic may wish to stroll up to the picturesque old R. Damiette to the Gothic church of St Ouen.] Return to the cathedral square.

Head down the R. du GROSSE HORLOGE to Rouen's famous landmark, the large ornamental clock set over a Renaissance gatehouse and its adjoining fourteenth-century belfry tower. Cross R. Jeanne d'Arc for the old marketplace and the modern CHURCH OF ST JOAN OF ARC. Consecrated in 1979, it can hold its own with Rouen's medieval glories. From the R. du Gros Horloge (good fish restaurant on your right) you catch a first glimpse of a curving slate roof, sloping almost to ground level and broken here and there by 'eyelid' windows, overhung by the slate and reminiscent of slender fish shapes. Sweeping round in a sinuous curve, the roof, with its remarkable fish-tail 'tower', extends beyond the church to provide the roofing for a cluster of market stalls. The modest entrance door is approached from a pillared remembrance gallery with a dedication by André Malraux to St Joan carved on its walls. To the left of the entrance stands a statue of the saint and beyond rise paved and stepped gardens which give a dramatic view of the varying planes, curves and levels of the church/market complex. Inside, the curve of the timbers carrying the roof is securely anchored by sturdily elegant iron tie rods; low-backed pale wood pews curve round to embrace altar and lectern. Beyond rises the majestic glass north wall, set with a ravishingly beautiful sequence of sixteenth-century stained glass from the old church of St Vincent, destroyed by bombing in 1944.

From the old market, the R. de Grosne leads to the Ave Gustave Flaubert and the museum of the great Rouen-born novelist (1821-80); the R. de la Pie to the museum-birthplace of Pierre Corneille (1606-84), France's first great tragic dramatist; a street from the SE corner to the Place de la Pucelle and the magnificent Gothic-Renaissance Bourghteroulde (pronounced 'Bootrood') Mansion (now a bank) - wall decorations in its beautiful courtyard depict the meeting between Francis I and Henry VIII at the 'Field of the Cloth of Gold' in 1520. Returning to the Gros Horloge, take the R. Thouret for the superbly ornate façade (1508-26) of the Palais de Justice. In the twelfth century the site was occupied by a Jewish synagogue (London's first Jewish community was settled, *c.* 1100, from Rouen). Through the courtyard, a pedestrian precinct leads across the R. Ganterie (left for half-timbered houses in R. des Bons Enfants) and the busy R. Thiers to the MUSÉE DES BEAUX-ARTS. The pearl of this outstanding gallery, the *Virgin Amongst the Virgins*, by the Flemish master Gerhardt David (1520s) is displayed in its own rotunda at the top of the main staircase. A ground-floor gallery is devoted to the Rouen artist Emile Blanche (1861-1942), portraitist of famous literary contemporaries such as Jean Cocteau. Other masterpieces include works by Veronese, Caravaggio, Velasquez, Poussin, Dufy and Duchamp Villon.

The entrance ticket here also entitles you also to visit Le Secq des Tournelles Museum (16 centuries of wrought iron-work); the Church of St Godard (fine wooden roof and outstanding stained glass); and the ceramics museum, all nearby. The Musée des Antiquités (Limoges enamels and Nottingham alabasters notable), on the R. Beauvoisine, is somewhat remote from the central tour. In the R. du Donjon (en route for the railway station from the Musée des Beaux-Arts), stands the Tour Jeanne d'Arc, the thirteenth-century tower where Joan was shown the instruments of torture.

CAEN

Alençon (via Sées) and neighbouring forests		220 km (137 mi) or 240 km (157 mi) (round trip with variants)
Bayeux		27 km (17 mi)
Honfleur		58 km (36 mi)
Trouville-Deauville		43 km (27 mi)
Mont-St-Michel	*St Malo	122 km (76 mi)
Rouen	*Dieppe	126 km (78 mi)
Fougères	*St Malo	126 km (78 mi)

Castle; Abbaye aux Hommes; Abbaye aux Dames; Normandy Beaches (D-Day landings).

Although the name is Celtic in origin (from a word meaning 'battlefield'), Caen first became important in 1060 when Duke William of Normandy began building the castle. Not yet thirty, 1.85 m (6 ft) tall and a noted warrior, he had flouted Church law by marrying his distant cousin Matilda of Flanders. Having been excommunicated after five years of living in sin, the couple promised, as penance, to found two churches. The results were the Abbayes aux Hommes and aux Femmes at Caen. From William's conquest of England in 1066 to the loss of the duchy under King John in 1204 (*Château Gaillard), Normandy and England were closely linked. Many an English church was built with stone from the famous quarries at Caen. Following Henry V's victory at Agincourt in 1415 (Caen fell two years later) Normandy was returned to English rule for some 30 years. In 1432 the English regent John, Duke of Bedford, founded Caen's university. During the sixteenth century Caen became a leading merchant city.

During the eighteenth century Caen became popular with the English and quite a large expatriate community grew up

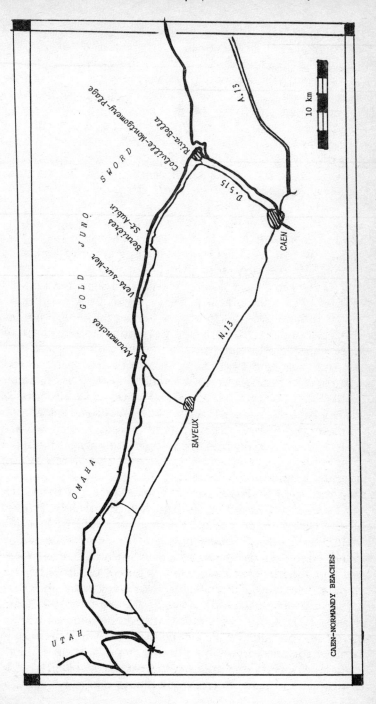

CAEN–NORMANDY BEACHES

here. In the 1830s 'Beau' Brummel, having fled here to escape his English creditors, became English consul for a time. During World War II Caen was a key point in the defences against Germany and was virtually obliterated in the Allied offensive and German counter-attack of June-July 1944. Yet the monuments survived and the rebuilding is good.

The S.I., the natural starting point for your tour, is housed in a restored sixteenth-century Renaissance merchant's mansion, the Hôtel d'Escoville (explore the ornate courtyard). Across the square stands the thirteenth-century church of St Pierre. The spire and nave roof, damaged in the 1944 bombardment, have both been restored. The W. porch with its rose window is in the Flamboyant style while the interior, notably the Renaissance E. end, is luxuriously ornate.

Duke William's CASTLE, opposite St Pierre, was enlarged in the twelfth century, from which period date the massive outer walls; the citadel was restored following extensive war damage. Within the precincts are the medieval Chapel of St George and the twelfth-century Exchequer building. Another medieval building, formerly the governor's house, contains the Normandy Museum with its displays of local life and craft and nineteenth-century social history. Across the castle grounds stand the fourteenth-century Porte des Champs ('Field Gate') and the elegant 1970s Musée des Beaux-Arts. It holds masterpieces by Rogier van der Weyden, Tintoretto, Veronese and Rubens, as well as numerous French works, among which are paintings by Boudin, Bonnard and Dufy; a major collection of engravings and etchings; porcelain, furniture and tapestries.

Returning to St Pierre, make your way E. to the OLD PORT with its pleasure craft, and the N. to Holy Trinity church, formerly the abbey church of the ABBAYE AUX FEMMES, standing in the Place de la Reine Mathilde. The towers have suffered from nineteenth-century restoration work but the immense nave remains one of the triumphs of Norman Romanesque architecture, with its great arches and grotesquely carved capitals. Two Romanesque chapels give off the N. transept; in the nineteenth century the matching pair off the S. transept were replaced by a single beautiful Gothic chapel, now the chapter house. Steps lead down to the eleventh-century crypt with its close-packed columns and low-groined vaulting. Above, in the chancel, the black marble

slab of Mathilde's tomb (desecrated during the Wars of Religion and the Revolution) can be seen set into the floor.

Now take the R. des Chanoines back to St Pierre and thence, past two sixteenth-century half-timbered houses, to the interesting double-naved church of St Sauveur with its wooden vault. The third right turn after the church, R. aux Fromages, invites a pleasant detour up a half-timbered street to the eighteenth-century Place St Sauveur. Alternatively, carry straight on to the distant towers of the ABBAYE AUX HOMMES, abbey church of St Étienne.

The Abbey was dedicated by Duke William in 1086, the year his Domesday survey of England was completed and the year before his death. The stark W. front, with its three Romanesque portals and slender flanking towers, embodies the uncompromising strength of the Norman style, set off by the thirteenth-century spires and echoed by the virtually unadorned and massive colonnades of the nave. The nave vaulting was done about 1130 and the Gothic chancel about

80 years later. The lantern tower was restored in the seventeenth century. A slab in front of the altar marks the tomb of the duke, desecrated in the 1560s and the 1790s when the mob threw bones found there into the River Orne. Before leaving St Étienne, make your way to the Esplanade Louvel or the Place Louis Guillouard to admire the pinnacles and buttresses which adorn the chapels radiating from the apse. The first abbot was the Italian churchman Lanfranc, who supervised the building works begun in the 1060s before becoming William's archbishop of Canterbury in 1070. The present conventual buildings (entrance from the Esplanade Louvel) date from the early eighteenth century and now house Caen's town hall. The wood carvings, staircases and striking views of the church make this a guided tour worth considering.

Twenty minutes (by car) from the centre of Caen lies the pleasant coast resort of RIVA BELLA with its fine sandy beaches. Once dotted with ruined block houses and wrecked military hardwear, this was the western extremity of the NORMANDY LANDINGS and of 'Sword Beach' in the British sector. Next to Riva Bella along the coast is Colleville Montgomery Plage, its name changed to commemorate the great British commander. Following the coast road brings you to St Aubin sur Mer and the beginning of Juno Beach, the Canadian sector. After another seven or eight miles you re-enter the British sector of Gold Beach at Asnelles. Just after Arromanches-les-Bains a left turn along the D.516 leads to Bayeux.

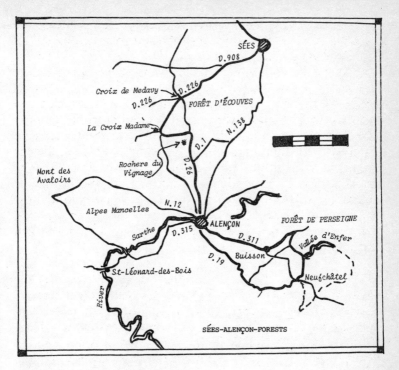

SÉES-ALENÇON-FORESTS

SÉES – ALENÇON –
FORÊT D'ÉCOUVES –
FORÊT DE PERSEIGNE

Route: round trip from Caen, see sketch map
Distance: 220 km (137 mi) (via Sées)
   240 km (157 mi) including neighbouring forests
Sées cathedral; lace manufacture and museum, Alençon;
forest walks.

This trip focuses on country pleasures rather than historic
sites, though there are those too. You can either spend a long
summer's day roaming the beautiful glades of oak and beech
and the stands of spruce and pine in the forests of Écouves
and Perseigne; or combine a forest picnic with a visit to a
charming little cathedral town or a famous old lace centre.
With the aid of the sketch map and good road map you can
plan your own route, or follow the one recommended.

SÉES, FORÊT D'ÉCOUVES

Entering Sées along the N.158 from Argentan make straight for the CATHEDRAL. The precincts are surrounded by pleasant seventeenth/eighteenth-century town houses, such as the old bishop's palace. The thirteenth-century W. front of the Cathedral is unfortunately spoilt by ungainly sixteenth-century buttressing of the large central porch, a reminder that even medieval master masons did not build for eternity. The handsome proportions of the Norman-Gothic nave are set off by an unusual frieze above. The chancel and transepts are lit by a clerestory with some attractive thirteenth-century stained glass.

The N.138 is the direct road for Alençon via the FORÊT D'ÉCOUVES. Leave Sées by the D.908 and just beyond Les Choux take the D.226 on the left. In August 1944 the region saw fierce fighting; today herds of deer and roebuck roam the woods in peace (except during the winter hunting season!). At the Medavy crossroads a tank monument commemorates the French 2nd Armoured Division; nearby there is an old milestone and a viewing platform commanding fine landscape PANORAMAS. A similar vantage point will be found a couple of miles further on at La Croix Madame. There is a number of blazed walks hereabouts through the pines.

At the crossroads two miles along the D.204 turn right to the Rochers du Vignage, a renowned beauty spot. From here you can either continue along the D.26 for Alençon or turn left at the D.1 beyond the Rochers for the N.138 back to Sées and thence to Caen.

ALENÇON

The D.26 brings you in along the R. d'Argentan. Turn left on the Boulevard de Strasbourg for the Place Général de Gaulle. If you have bypassed the Forêt d'Écouves trip and are coming from Sées direct the N.138 leads straight to the Place. Now take the R. St Blaise past the Chapel of Ste Thérèse (Martin); next door is the house where the saint was born in 1873. The Church of Nôtre Dame will be on your left. The ornate central porch (early 1500s) and the Flamboyant buttresses are impressive. The 1400s interior was spoilt by eighteenth-century rebuilding but there is some attractive sixteenth-century glass. The restored fifteenth-century Maison Ozé nearby houses a small museum (a miscellaneous collection including Gallo-Roman archaeology and exhibits from Cambodia). Take the Grande Rue to the crossroads, then turn right up the R. du Château for the Place Foch with the law courts, the town hall and the MUSÉE DES BEAUX-ARTS ET DE LA DENTELLE (lace). The paintings on the ground and first floors are mostly by French masters from the sixteenth to nineteenth centuries, among them Philippe de Champagne, Vigée-Lebrun, Géricault and Boudin. The LACE MUSEUM in the upper galleries has displays showing the manufacture of the renowned Alençon needlepoint lace (originally developed in imitation of Venetian lace) and superb examples of work from the peak period of the seventeenth and eighteenth centuries. The law courts are housed in the surviving parts of the old CASTLE of the counts and dukes of Alençon; notice the late-1300s Tour du Chevalier and the massive fifteenth-century gateway. In the 1570s Duke Francis I (younger son of King Henry III) was a suitor of Elizabeth I of England. Pockmarked and sadly misshapen, her 'little frog', as she called him, charmed the Queen by his wit and gallantry.

West of Alençon lies the wooded and undulating landscape of the Forêt de Multonne, the Forêt de Pail and the Valley of the Sarthe, known locally and rather optimistically as the Mancelles Alps. Enquire at the S.I. for recommended routes. Or take a drive in the FORÊT DE PERSEIGNE. From Place Foch follow the R. du Château and its continuations over the River Sarthe and bear right in the Place de la Division Leclerc until you come to a 'Y' junction and the D.311, direction Mamers. At Le Buisson turn left along the D.236 for a couple of miles; a hairpin right leads you deeper into the forest and the Rond de Croix Pergeline. From here you can turn left for the picturesque Vallée d'Enfer ('Hell Valley'), with picnic areas and marked walks below a hill-top gazebo – or right for a little forest road to the hamlet of Neufchâtel and the road back to Alençon.

BAYEUX

Route (Caen): N.13
Distance: 27 km (17 mi)
Bayeux tapestry; cathedral; British Military Cemetery.

Approaching along the N.13 turn left at the ring road and follow the Boulevards Montgomery and Sadi Carnot for the Cathedral. Alternatively, bear left from Sadi Carnot along Boulevard Leclerc and General Fabian Ware for the BRITISH MILITARY CEMETERY and the Memorial Museum to the Battle of Normandy before taking the R. de Verdun for the Cathedral and the nearby S.I.

An ancient Gaulish settlement of the Bajocasses, the place was occupied by the Romans and about AD 900 by the Norsemen. Rollo, Normandy's first duke, married the governor of Bayeux's daughter and their son William Longsword, the second duke, was born here. In the 1070s William the Conqueror's half-brother Odo, the warrior bishop of Bayeux and prominent in the conquest of England, founded the Cathedral. On 7 June 1944 Bayeux became the first French town to be liberated from German occupation.

The CATHEDRAL represents a combination of Norman Romanesque and Gothic styles of the finest quality; the tower added in the fifteenth century was unfortunately restored in the nineteenth. The Romanesque towers at the W. end have thirteenth-century spires, the columns of the nave and the eleventh-century crypt are classic examples of Norman work. Within the beautiful thirteenth-century stonework of the choir observe the elegant sixteenth-century stalls. The paintings of the martyrdom of St Thomas à Becket inside the S. transept are nineteenth-century, the other scenes dating from the fifteenth. Leave by the door in the S. aisle to admire the flying buttresses and the thirteenth-century relief in the tympanum over the S. transept porch depicting Becket's martyrdom. Other outstanding thirteenth-century Gothic work can be seen in the Chapter House.

Across the road from the S. transept stands the former episcopal palace and, nearby in the R. de Nesmond, the late seventeenth-century building which now houses the BAYEUX TAPESTRY. This unique work (not a true tapestry) comprises a wool-embroidered linen scroll 70.34 m (231 ft) long and some 0.5 m (20 in) deep and was perhaps commissioned for his cathedral by Bishop Odo. The old French name, '*Tapisserie de la reine Mathilde*', reflects the now discredited tradition that it was worked by Queen Matilda. Most scholars now agree it was in fact worked by English women (possibly nuns). Anglo-Saxon embroidery had a European reputation and the work is of the highest quality. Known to have been in the Cathedral at least since the fifteenth century, it narrowly escaped destruction by Revolutionaries in the 1790s. A decade later it was sent on travelling exhibition round France on the orders of Napoleon as propaganda promotion for his intended invasion of England.

Somewhat in the manner of a strip cartoon, the tapestry tells the story of the Norman conquest (from the Norman point of view) in narrative panel scenes, accompanied by a running commentary of Latin captions. Among the many famous scenes, Harold of England is shown swearing loyalty to Duke William of Normandy (23). Historians have long debated the nature of this oath, even whether it took place; the tapestry's depiction bears testimony to the power of visual record in propaganda. Also notice the death of King Edward the Confessor (26); the appearance of Halley's comet (32); the building of the fleet (36); the Normans establishing their beach-head near Pevensey, assembling prefabricated wooden forts, etc.; and of course the Battle of Hastings and the death of Harold. One of the most famous artefacts to survive from the Middle Ages, the tapestry tells a compelling narrative and is packed with detail. The top and bottom borders are embellished with fabulous monsters, scenes of everyday life and fables and proverbs.

From the Tapestry building you may care to visit the LACE-MAKING centre on the R. St Jean and the BARON GÉRARD MUSEUM which lies between the Cathedral and the S.I.; its treasures include old master paintings, tapestries and a collection of Bayeux lace (seventeenth to nineteenth centuries). You can either return direct to Caen or take the D.516 from the northern ring road for Arromanches and the coast road along the Beaches ('Gold', 'Juno' and 'Sword') of the British and Canadian sectors during the Normandy landings. For the American sector of Omaha Beach turn left at Arromanches.

HONFLEUR

Route (Caen): A.13 or N.175 to Pont l'Évêque, then D.579
Distance: 60 km (37.5 mi)
Old fishing port; wooden church of St Catherine; Boudin museum.

The D.579 brings you in along the R. de la République to the Old Port. Keep an early lookout for parking as the old town tends to get rather congested.

Fortified in the Middle Ages, Honfleur fell twice to the English during the Hundred Years War, providing a disembarkation port for Edward III's armies in the 1360s and an important harbour for English Normandy (1418-49). In 1603 a flotilla commanded by Samuel Champlain sailed from here for the colonization of Canada and the founding of Quebec.

The inner OLD PORT, constructed in the late seventeenth century, with its lofty old timber and slate-roofed houses (Quai Ste Catherine) and packed with jostling pleasure cruisers and fishing smacks, is one of Europe's most picturesque waterfronts. There is a quality restaurant or you can linger at one of the bistros or cafés. Stroll up the Place Thiers to find the S.I. On the Quai St Étienne stands the Musée du Vieux Honfleur, which incorporates the old St Stephen's Church and comprises collections of maritime and local history (in a separate building nearby). Continue on towards the outer or Avant Port and cross the swing bridge to La Lieutenance (the old Governor's House). This is a curious conglomeration with oriel corner turrets, a niche statue of the Virgin and Child, and one of the town's old gates incorporated in its structure. To one side is the quaint Old Port, to the other the Avant Port, the centre of Honfleur's present activity as a commercial and fishing port (good restaurants here on the Quai de la Quarantine and Quai des Passagers).

From the Lieutenance visit the fairy-tale CHURCH OF ST CATHERINE. Built after the expulsion of the English by local shipwrights, St Catherine's is entirely timber-built (remarkable in Europe outside Scandinavia). Opposite the W. end stands the BELFRY building. Massive timber struts rise as buttresses through its wood shingle roof to support a square tower with louvred openings, topped by a helm roof from which soars an octagonal spire. The W. end of the Church itself creates a unique impression. Two gabled porches, linked by a little cloister, project from the half-timbered wall; above rise the massive gables of the double nave behind. At ground level can be seen the penthouse roofs of the side aisles. Within, massive timber pillars, cross-beams and king posts support the curving timber inner roofs of the naves; above the aisle walls cunningly contrived Gothic-style square windows provide a clerestory, while at the E. end three larger windows frame the high altar. Half-timbered panels, hanging paintings, banners and statues punctuate the lines of this masterpiece of the carpenter's art.

Take the R. de l'Homme de Bois for the MUSÉE BOUDIN in the Place Erik Satie. Both Satie the composer (1886-1925; born at 90 R. Haute) and Eugène Boudin (1824-98) the painter were natives of Honfleur. Boudin, who worked at Deauville and Trouville as well as Honfleur, and is noted for his choppy seascapes and fashionable beach scenes, anticipated the Impressionists in painting direct from nature, *en plein air*, and probably introduced Monet to the idea. Honfleur itself became a favourite haunt of the Impressionists and has remained popular with artists, especially amateurs, ever since. Raoul Dufy worked here and he, like Monet, Jongkind and many others, is represented in the museum, though Boudin's work naturally predominates.

From the museum a beautiful half-mile walk up the Côte de Grace hill brings you to a viewing platform with a grand PANORAMA across to Le Havre and the Seine estuary. Over the centuries the little church of Nôtre Dame de Grace here has been the chapel for Honfleur's seafarers. Every Whit Sunday and Monday the Honfleur Seamen's Festival witnesses the Blessing of the Sea, a mass at Nôtre Dame and processions of seamen and children bearing model ships down to the beach.

It is possible to combine a trip to Honfleur with an afternoon on the beaches of Trouville-Deauville some 15 km (10 mi) along the D.513.

TROUVILLE-DEAUVILLE

Route (Caen): N.175 to Pont l'Évêque, then N.177
Distance: 43 km (27 mi)
Attractive seaside resort.

Of these twin resorts, divided by the River Touques and fashionable since the mid-1800s, DEAUVILLE is perhaps the smarter. Attractions include the Touques race course and the Hippodrome de Clairefontaine, the Port Deauville Marina and the old 'Summer' and 'Winter' casinos. On the front are the Pompeian Baths and the Bar Soleil while the front itself, as at Trouville, is lined by the wooden-planked promenade LES PLANCHES – a place to see and be seen. Stroll out along the marina's breakwater or turn right for the elegant Boulevard Eugène Cornuche. Turning left brings you to the river and thence to TROUVILLE. Now considered a little downmarket, Trouville was first 'discovered' back in the 1830s when the Paris smart set took up sea bathing. A generation later fashion moved across the river, where speculators were laying out select residential villas. The beach here is a bit busier, but Trouville has an old casino, an S.I. near the ferry and a pretty little MUSEUM with paintings by Boudin, Isabey, who stayed here, and sundry others, as well as its PLANCHES and beautiful sands. The POINTE DE LA CORNICHE at the end of town has a vantage point for beautiful panoramas.

After a morning on the beach you could consider the 15-km (10-mi) trip to *Honfleur. The road, called the Normandy Corniche and passing such resorts as Villerville, is a magnificent scenic drive.

ST MALO-DINARD

Angers	189 km (118 mi)
Carnac	209 km (131 mi) or 179 km (112 mi)
Dinan	22 km (14½ mi)
Dol-de-Bretagne	24 km (15 mi)
Fougères	75 km (49 mi)
Mont-St-Michel	52 km (32½ mi)
Rennes	69 km (44 mi)

Facing each other across the mouth of the Rance estuary, the historic sea port of St Malo and the pretty seaside resort of Dinard make a good base for a touring holiday.

Thanks to a combination of geography, history and civil engineering, St Malo presents the unusual spectacle of a busy sea port with its town (on a rocky promontory) seaward of the harbour and docks. To reach the old town direct from the Gare Maritime you skirt the Jacques Cartier dock to the Ave Louis Martin, where you will find the S.I.

In the sixth century the St Malo promontory with its outlying island, the Île du Grand Bé, linked by a causeway, was the site of an abbey where the Welsh saint Maclou is said to have found refuge. The port grew and for centuries was to be a base for Breton privateers operating against French and English shipping. One of the town's most famous sons was Jacques Cartier (d. 1557), who reconnoitred the coast of Canada (the name he gave to the country, though it was actually the Huron Indian word for 'village'). In the 1760s the navigator Bougainville established a short-lived settlement in the Falkland Islands which he named Les Malouines. The Spaniards expelled the French but retained the name as Las Malvinas. Probably the most famous Malouin was the writer Chateaubriand (1768-1848), interred at his own wish in a granite tomb on the ÎLE DU GRAND BÉ.

In August 1944 virtually the entire old town was demolished in two weeks of fighting following the Normandy landings of the Allied invasion of German-dominated Europe. Apart from the ramparts, the town as we see it today is the product of loving post-war restoration and rebuilding.

You enter the OLD TOWN through the double gateway of St Vincent (also called the Grande Porte) which leads, by the Grande Rue, to the Church (formerly cathedral) of ST VINCENT. The S. transept was utterly destroyed in 1944 but much of the old building survives. The central tower is fifteenth-century, the massive nave pillars twelfth and the vaulting Gothic. The CHOIR (early 1300s) is especially beautiful and the restored church is lit by some outstanding modern stained glass.

The RAMPARTS were established in the twelfth century but continually improved and refortified. The wall walk, decidedly hard work on a windy day, offers splendid views over the town and out to sea. The fort on the headland dates from the 1680s and was designed by the distinguished military engineer the Marquis de Vauban. The CHÂTEAU DE LA DUCHESSE ANNE projecting from the NE corner of the ramparts retains much of its fifteenth-century keep, now housing the extensive local history museum. Adjacent is the AQUARIUM, a gallery of more than 130 m (400 ft) with scores of tanks built into the old ramparts skirting the Place Vauban.

St Malo's GRANDE PLAGE is a fine beach stretching up the coast to Parame and S. of the harbour lies the pretty resort of St Servan sur Mer (in fact on the Rance estuary) with a marina, three beaches and a superb cliff walk round the CORNICHE D'ALETH. The eighteenth-century fort here was greatly extended and modernized by the Germans during World War II, with a warren of underground passages linking blockhouses and service quarters. To the south the Solidor Tower, on its own little promontory, houses the International Museum of Cape Horn navigation, with ship models, dioramas and tableaux depicting shipboard conditions from the 1500s to the early 1900s.

Many delightful boating trips, notably down the Rance estuary, sail from St Malo (check times at the S.I.). For anyone interested in engineering or in alternative sources of energy the RANCE USINE MAREMOTRICE, Tidal Power Station, is a must. The D.168 road linking St Malo to Dinard runs across a 750-m (760-yd)-long dam which converts the lower estuary into a vast reservoir. Opened in 1966, the plant utilizes tidal surge to generate a potential output of 550 million kw per year. Twenty-four AC generators are housed in the body of the dam; an adjacent lock permits continued navigation up-river to light shipping, while sluices control the water level behind the dam to best advantage. There is a permanent explanatory exhibition and occasional access to a viewing gallery in the generator room. Not the least interesting thing about the plant is the fact that there were tidal mills on this stretch of the Rance in the Middle Ages.

DINARD

An obscure fishing village until its 'discovery' by a rich American in the 1850s, Dinard's mild climate and beautiful bay soon made it a favourite retreat with the English. By 1900 it was a smart resort with a British consul ministering to the expatriate community – among them, for a time, the family of the boy T.E. Lawrence. In the 1920s the casino behind the Grande Plage was much patronized by the international set.

The sea-front is lined with luxury hotels; the beach, also called the Place de l'Écluse, is in a deep bay. Westwards you can walk round to the Pointe des Etêtes with a cliff walk along to Plage St Enogat. Eastwards lies the promontory of the POINTE DU MOULINET, which commands wide vistas; far away to the west you can see the red granite cliffs of Cap Frehel 32 km (20 mi) distant; to the east, across the Rance estuary, the fortress-like profile of old St Malo.

Dinard's AQUARIUM AND MARINE MUSEUM stands on the R. Levavasseur overlooking the Rance estuary. Southwards from here the Promenade du Clair de Lune makes a beautiful walk to the Plage du Prieure (with the ruins of the medieval Priory chapel). Still further eastwards lies the expensive residential area of La Vicomte. From Dinard as from St Malo you can take delightful boat trips along the coast and down the Rance. Enquire at the S.I.

ANGERS

Route (St Malo): N.137 to Rennes, D.163/D.963-N.23
Distance: 189 km (118 mi)
Castle; Apocalypse tapestries; Hospital of St John.

Standing on the River Maine just above its confluence with the Loire, Angers was the historic home of the Counts of Anjou who, in the person of Henry II (d. 1189), founded the Angevin Plantagenet dynasty of English kings. It is the capital of the old province of Anjou and also the home of the liqueur Cointreau, created here in 1849 (and liable to be served by the wine glass).

The N.23 brings you in along Ave Pasteur to the Place Général Leclerc. After skirting the square and its public gardens turn left along the Boulevard Bessoneau and Boulevard Maréchal Foch then right at the Boulevard du Roi René for the CASTLE, a grimly business-like fortress which makes a contrast to the sugar-candy pleasure palaces of the Loire.

An earlier castle on the rocky riverside site was the base for Count Fulk the Black ('Nerra', d. 1040), who claimed descent from the Devil. The turbulent Angevin counts expanded their territories and then in the 1150s Henry of Anjou became king of England, duke of Normandy and lord of Aquitaine. More than half of France was ranged against the kings in Paris. The loss of Normandy in 1204 (*Château Gaillard), followed by the French occupation of Anjou, curbed Angevin power. The title Count (later Duke) of Anjou was reserved for sons of the French kings. The present castle was completed in the 1230s under King Saint Louis IX, a sorry fate for the fortress of the Devil's Brood of Angevins.

The castle area (apart from the riverside, now lined with houses) is surrounded by a massive pentagon of curtain walls and 17 massive drum towers, once all the same height as the lofty Tour du Moulin ('Windmill Tower'). During the sixteenth-century Wars of Religion the Castle held for a time for the Protestants: the towers were dismantled to wall level on the orders of King Henry III. The threatening aspect of the fortress is somewhat lightened by the decorative bandings of slate, sandstone and granite.

Crossing the drawbridge, you may glimpse some of the deer which roam the rock-hewn moat. The gatehouse is defended by two towers, a formation repeated at the SE corner where a second drawbridge once led out from the gate there. Formal gardens are laid out within the precinct. To your right is a fifteenth-century chapel, built above a Gothic Angevin vault, for Yolande, wife of Count Louis II. Adjoining it is the turreted and pinnacled Châtelet, or Petit Château, gatehouse of a residence built by Duke René (1409-80), 'Good King René', titular king of Naples (*Aix-en-Provence). Beyond is the modern gallery housing the APOCALYPSE TAPESTRIES, a medieval series of 70 woven panels depicting scenes from The Book of Revelation, 'The Apocalypse'.

The vast frieze originally comprised 90 horizontal panels, in two rows punctuated by seven vertical panels showing Worthies of the Church. It extended some 160 m (470 ft) and was about 5.5 m (18 ft) deep. The work was commissioned by Count Louis I (d. 1384), brother of King Charles V, and completed under Count Louis II. The tapestries were woven in the Paris workshops of Nicholas Bataille from cartoons by Hennequin of Bruges, a court painter, who based his designs on two illuminated manuscripts in the royal library (they still survive). Running borders depict a flowery mead below and angels among the clouds above. Thus St John's harrowing vision of the Last Things unfolds between Earth and Heaven. The panels' background colours are alternatively red and blue. Here and there can be seen the letters 'L', 'M' and 'Y', for the two counts Louis and their wives Marie and Yolande. Thirty dyes were used and although the colours have faded somewhat the austere designs, punctuated by many-headed monsters, haloed saints, showers of blood and stars, are awesome.

On the death of Duke René (1480) the great work was transferred from the Castle to the Cathedral, where it remained for some 250 years. The 'polite' taste of the eighteenth century rejected medieval art as barbarous and the Cathedral authorities put the tapestries up for auction. There was no buyer and for a century the masterpiece mouldered. Bits were thriftily cut out to provide rugs and carpeting, and a large section was used as winter covering for fruit trees. In the 1840s a devoted scholar bought the surviving sections for just 300 francs and began the job of restoration.

The Castle contains two other outstanding tapestry collections (fifteenth and eighteenth centuries) in the Governor's

and the Royal Lodgings which abut the SE curtain wall.
Leaving the Castle take the R. Toussaint (S.I. nearby) towards a right turning for the late-1400s Logis Barrault
mansion which houses the MUSÉE DES BEAUX-ARTS. Its
treasures include a large collection of the work of the
nineteenth-century neo-classical sculptor David d'Angers
(Jean-Pierre David); a Madonna and Child by the fourteenth-
century Sienese painter Sassetta; a famous fifteenth-century
anonymous portrait of Agnes Sorel (mistress of King Charles
VII) and works by many other French masters, among them
Géricault and Ingres.

The Cathedral of St Maurice (near the museum), dating
from the twelfth century, is a stark, somewhat awkward
building. Of its three towers, the central one in Renaissance
style was added in the 1540s; the spacious but aisleless nave
retains much of its original (thirteenth-century) glass; the
rose windows date from the fifteenth century. Beyond the E.
end the shopping street R. St Aubin runs up to the Church of
St Martin with its ancient belfry, while the R. Lenepveu
(good shops here too) takes you to the Place du Ralliement,
beyond which lies the Logis Pince. This heavily restored
sixteenth-century building contains collections on archaeology and of objets d'art and Japanese prints. From the
Cathedral's W. end a stepped street leads down to the Pont de
Verdun across the Maine. Continue along R. Beaurepair to
the Place de la Laiterie: good shops, sixteenth-century town
houses and the twelfth-century porch of La Trinité church.
On your right is the École Militaire, the academy where,
improbably enough, the young Arthur Wesley (later Welles-
ley) trained as a soldier. Years later, a grateful sovereign was
to create him 1st Duke of Wellington. Take the Boulevard
Arago for the ANCIEN HÔPITAL DE ST JEAN, founded by
Henry II of England in penance for the murder of St Thomas
à Becket. The original granary (old wine presses on display)
and cloister are open to the public, as is the old dispensary.
The beautifully vaulted Salle des Malades ('sick ward',
1180s), a noble three-aisled interior, houses the 10-piece
Chant du Monde ('Song of the World') tapestry (1957-60). It
is the last work of Jean Lurçat, who, at the Aubusson factory,
led the French revival of tapestry as an art form. The bold
colours and jagged lines of the '*Chant*' well represent his style
of modernism.

CARNAC

Routes (St Malo):
(a) longer, but better roads and simpler to map-read: N.137 to Rennes, N.24 to Ploërmel, N.166 to Vannes, N.165 to Auray, D.768 (direction Quiberon) then D.186 for Carnac
Distance: 209 km (131 mi)
(b) shorter, more interesting, but on minor roads: N.137 to Châteauneuf, D.29/N.176 to Dinan, D.766 to Caulnes, cross the N.12 and continue along the D.166 to St-Méen-le-Grand then to Ploërmel and so on to Carnac
Distance: 179 km (112 mi)
Either way, 3 hours is good driving.

Renowned prehistoric site; scenic drive across Brittany; good beach.

A long excursion for an early start on a fine day (April to September). But then, the Dinan route is a lovely drive through often wooded country and either way your destination is one of Europe's most intriguing neolithic sites, with the added bonus of a pine-fringed beach set about with elegant hotels, cafés and restaurants.

About 3 km (1½ mi) short of Carnac the D.186 makes a fork with the D.119 which you now follow. The approach to Carnac lies through an astonishing landscape of ancient standing stones (in Breton '*menhirs*', meaning 'long stones'), up to 4 m (12 ft) in height and more than 2700 in number. Just beyond the fork, off the road to the right, stands the Moustoir Tumulus. The earth mound covers a megalithic chamber tomb. The word 'megalith', from the Greek meaning 'great stone', is generally used for these prehistoric stone monuments of various types to be found in a great arc from the north of Scotland, through Ireland, western Britain and Brittany down to Spain and Malta. You are about to see many more. About a mile beyond the tumulus you take another right fork (D.196) for the ALIGNMENTS OF MENEC.

Here some 1100 stones are set in 11 rows stretching about 1 km (⅜ mi) – the distance between the outermost rows being 100 m (330 ft) – in a NE direction roughly parallel to

the road. The alignment is closed by a semi-circular formation of 70 menhirs in and around the village of Menec. From
the raising of the first stones in the 3rd millenium BC work at
Carnac continued intermittently for some 1300 years. A local
legend, paralleled at other European sites with megaliths,
held that they were petrified soldiers, who in this case had
been impiously pursuing a local saint by the name of Cornély.
Scholarly theories, more plausible perhaps but with scarcely
more evidence, have ranged from funerary monuments, to
ceremonial processional ways, to a massive calendrical in-
strument aligned on the sunrise at solstices and equinox to
help determine the times of religious ceremonies. Like
Stonehenge, the Carnac menhirs were once attributed to the
Celtic Druids – whose cult began centuries after the last stone
had been raised.

After your visit continue on the D.196 into Carnac for
coffee or lunch. A dog-leg crossing of the R. de St Cornély (he
of petrified army fame) brings you into the Ave Salines and
the right direction for the beach. The S.I. in the Ave des
Druides is rich in information on the scores of megalithic
monuments in the region. A week or two might be long
enough to see them all: I suggest you confine yourself to the
Menec alignment, already seen, and those of Kermario and
Kerlescan described below.

After an early start from St Malo you should have time for
an hour or two on the beach, either Carnac Plage or the
adjacent La Trinité Plage. The Miln-Le Rouzic Museum of
Prehistory, a short step from St Cornély's church, is closed
for lunch and there is nothing else of special historic interest
in Carnac. Leaving the town by the Ave du Rahic you come
to the ST MICHEL TUMULUS on your right just before
joining the D.118 for Auray. The great mound, 120 m (395
ft) long and 12 m (38 ft) high, has the little Chapel of St
Michael and a viewing table from which to identify the
landmarks of the PANORAMA landscape view. Within is a
number of megalithic burial chambers. You may not find an
English-speaking guide nor one who is especially knowledge-
able, but the 15-minute guided tour of this ancient place
opens the doors of the imagination. (Be prepared for a wait.)

Half a mile on turn right along the D.196 for the ALIGN-
MENT OF KERMARIO – 10 rows of menhirs stretching for
half a mile along the roadside. To the right is the Kercado

Tumulus, surmounted by a single menhir and containing a single fine chamber tomb. At the junction of the D.196 and D.186 (left for Auray) is the ALIGNMENT OF KERLES-CAN. Here a ring formation of 39 menhirs stands at the base of 13 rows of more than 500 stones aligned to the NE.

Although on leaving the irreverent may opine that once one has seen one standing stone one has seen the lot, the cumulative impact of these ancient, relentless lines, still discharging their long-forgotten purpose upon the landscape of the present, can be eerie – even a little unnerving.

DINAN

Route (Dinard): D.766
Distance: 22 km (14½ mi)
Château; clock tower; medieval-Renaissance streets and houses.

A dramatic old hill town, Dinan, with its old ramparts and half-timbered houses climbing up from the valley of the Rance to promenades and gardens, begs to be explored.

From Dinard you approach along the R. Gambetta to the Place Général Leclerc. Continue (ramparts on your left) along the R. Thiers to the large traffic interchange of Place Duclos. Turn left and then fork right up the wide R. du Marchix to the Place du Guesclin (parking), an urbane seventeenth/ eighteenth-century square with glimpses of the surrounding countryside below and some attractive cafés and restaurants. From the SW corner of the Place, the R. du Château leads to the late fourteenth-century CASTLE (closed Tuesdays) with its Coëtquen Tower and massive 30-m (100-ft)-high Donjon de la Duchesse Anne, now the local history museum. Return to R. du Château (right) for the Promenade de la Duchesse Anne. Below the town ramparts the River Rance swings away and back again towards the town to flow under a massive viaduct carrying the N.176 to Paris. The Promenade ends in the Jardin Anglais, former cemetery of St Sauveur's church. From the Gardens you have a bird's-eye view of the Old Port, now crowded with pleasure cruisers, and the reconstructed 'Gothic Bridge' away to the left.

Facing the W. front of the BASILICA OF ST SAUVEUR

admire the twelfth-century Romanesque porch and the Flamboyant fifteenth-century gable and window above; the contrast of styles continues in the interior. A grave monument in the N. transept contains the heart of the fourteenth-century Breton hero Bertrand du Guesclin. One of the side chapels contains a twelfth-century font, another a beautiful fifteenth-century window. In the left-hand corner of the Place, opposite the basilica, a narrow street leads to the R. de l'Orloge. Down to your left is the handsome columned 1500s Hotel Keratry housing the S.I. Continuing this way would bring you to the Place du Guesclin. Opposite is the TOUR DE L'ORLOGE with its fifteenth-century clock and a view over the town. With the S.I. behind you walk on down the R. de l'Orloge to the picturesque Place des Merciers, the projecting upper storeys of its old houses supported by great wooden pillars. From here the R. de l'Apport brings you to the Place des Cordeliers, with several old houses and the fifteenth-century gateway of a former convent. A short diversion down the Grande Rue leads to the Flamboyant-style Church of St Malo. Take the R. de la Lainerie for the most dramatic of all Dinan's old streets, the cobbled R. du Jerzual. Plunging down to the river, it winds between steeply gabled half-timbered houses with here and there a hoist projecting from an upper window or a louvred dovecote under the gable eaves. Many of the lower floors now accommodate craft studios. Through the JERZUAL GATE in the ramparts you are in the R. du Petit Fort – no. 24, Maison du Gouverneur, is an outstanding fifteenth-century house and the street continues its curving course down to the river with many another lovely building. You will reach the river bank at the Gothic Bridge, with a pleasant stroll along towards the Old Port and the towering viaduct. But be warned: the return journey is a real climb. If you decide to miss the river walk, return from the Maison du Gouverneur up the R. du Jerzual and turn left up the R. Haute Voie. Near the top you pass the fine Renaissance gateway to the old Beaumanoir Mansion and the charming courtyard beyond. Some 50 yards further on you are back in the R. de l'Orloge. Passing the clock tower and the S.I., turn right along the R. Ste Claire to regain the Place du Guesclin.

DOL-DE-BRETAGNE and MONT DOL

Route (St Malo): D.155 via Le Vivier-sur-Mer
Distance: 24 km (15 mi)
Picturesque and dramatic, the little town of Dol and the neighbouring Mont Dol (literally, 'Table Mount': Breton dol = 'table'), can be well explored in a comparatively short time: and you could combine the visit with one to *Mont-St-Michel.

Approaching from Le Vivier-sur-Mer you see MONT DOL on the left (D.123). Though barely 65 m (210 ft) high, the granite outcrop rising abruptly from the surrounding plain creates an eerie impression. Prehistoric animal bones (mammoth etc.) and flint tools have been found and local legend endows it with a still older mythical significance. Here, it is said, St Michael did battle with the Devil near the little chapel of Nôtre Dame de l'Espérance on the top. A series of declivities on the northern slope are supposedly the marks left by their combat. There are splendid PANORAMAS to Dol-de-Bretagne and out across the Bay to Mont-St-Michel (where, incidentally, the Devil lost the final round to Michael after a giant leap to the mountain in a vain attempt to escape his saintly opponent). There are some medieval wall paintings in the church at the bottom of the mount.

Entering DOL-DE-BRETAGNE along the D.155 you quickly find yourself in the square of ST SAMSON'S, formerly a cathedral. An earlier church was destroyed (*c.*1200) in John of England's campaign against his young nephew, Arthur of Brittany: the present thirteenth/fourteenth-century fortress-like building was made part of the town's defences. The fourteenth-century GREAT PORCH on the S. has the arms of Bishop Coueret (1405-59) and the thirteenth-century Little Porch also has his punning device of a heart ('*coeur*'). The interior, more than 100 m (328 ft) long, is both impressive and unusual for the detached side shafts of its columns. The tomb of Bishop James (d. 1504) was commissioned from two Florentine brothers, an unusually early example of Italian Renaissance art in Northern Europe. There are a sixteenth-century carved bishop's throne, a medieval wood statue of the Virgin (painted, nineteenth-century) above the high altar, fourteenth-century choir stalls and late thirteenth-century glass in the E. window. To the E. of the Cathedral, the Promenade de Douves' public gardens command beautiful views of Mont Dol. The sixteenth-century Treasury Building on the Cathedral Square has good local history displays. From the square walk down to the T-junction of the Grande Rue des Stuarts, lined by fine old houses from the Middle Ages to the seventeenth century.

Before leaving Dol visit the CHAMP DOLENT MENHIR, barely 2 km (1½ mi) away. Take the D.795 (direction Rennes); after the fork of the D.4 you will see a left turn. About 9 m (30 ft) high, it is one of the finest of all the standing stones of prehistoric Brittany.

FOUGÈRES

Route (St Malo): D.155
Distance: 80 km (50 mi)
Castle.

The D.155 brings you into town at a T-junction with the Boulevard de Rennes. Turn right for the CASTLE.

Once a frontier fortress of the duchy of Brittany, the castle now stands at the centre of the little town, which climbs the hillsides around it. Somehow, the great bastion retains an air of menacing strength. For the young T.E. Lawrence, whose holiday tours of the Welsh and French castles foreshadowed his university thesis on the Crusader castles of Syria, Fougères was 'quite above and beyond words'. At the time of his visit (1907) a good deal of restoration work had been done; the work has continued and today the great courtyard serves as an open-air theatre. A superb production of Hugo's *Les Misérables* mounted there in 1983 may have inspired the West End hit musical.

The castle was built on a peninsular formed by the River Nançon. A moat cut at the neck completed the encirclement and this is now the main river. An earlier fortress on the site was captured and destroyed (1166) by the neighbouring duke of Normandy (who as Henry II also happened to be king of England). But Raoul II, Lord of Fougères, quickly rebuilt. Parts of his twelfth-century work survive; the rest of the building dates from the thirteenth to the fifteenth centuries.

Begin with a circuit of the walls. From the Place Raoul II notice the projecting corbelled fourteenth-century Guibet turret in the centre of the N. rampart. The great pond formed by the river creates some magical reflections at night when the castle is floodlit. Right of the turret rises the thirteenth/fourteenth-century Gobelins tower at the base of a triangular outwork with a postern gate (to a fore-castle now demolished). Skirting the outwork you see the Mélusine Tower, rising 31 m (99 ft) from the rock. In the fourteenth century Fougères passed to the lords of Lusignan, who claimed descent from the mythical Mélusine, daughter of the Devil. Following the R. le Bouteillier you come to the fifteenth-century Surienne and Raoul towers, adapted as gun platforms. (Opposite is the Church of St Sulpice, 1400s-1700s but predominantly Flamboyant in style and containing a twelfth-century statue of the Virgin.) Next comes the thirteenth-century Cadran Tower and then the Gate of Nôtre Dame, the only one of four entrances through the old town ramparts to survive.

At the R. de la Pinterie turn sharp left for the main entrance to the castle and the guided tour of the interior. The wall walk, high above the moat and the inner courtyard of this massive fortress, is a dramatic experience. There is a little museum of bygones in the Raoul Tower (costume and shoes: Fougères has a long tradition of quality shoe manufacture) and an outstanding view from the top of the Mélusine Tower (75 steps).

Leaving the Castle, take the R. de la Pinterie with sections of the old ramparts (fifteenth-century Nichot Tower) and formal gardens. At the Place du Théâtre turn right and make your way up to the tree-shaded Place aux Arbres, SE of the castle on the former town ramparts, with the sixteenth-century Hôtel de Ville and the Church of St Leonard (fifteenth/sixteenth centuries). Descend the Escalier de la Duchesse Anne to the river and over the bridge to the charming old Place du Marchix. The picturesque old houses continue down the R. du Nançon, which brings you back to the castle area.

Three km (2 mi) out of Fougères, NE along the D.177, lie the wide-spreading beech woods of the FORÊT DE FOUGÈRES, with delightful walks and megalithic stone monuments and standing stones (signposted).

MONT-ST-MICHEL

Route (St Malo): D.155/D.797 to Pontorson, D.976
Distance: 52 km (32.5 mi)
Route (Caen): N.175 to Avranches, then Pontaubault
and D.75
Distance: 122 km (76 mi)
One of those places which actually outdo their reputation,
Mont-St-Michel, despite the crowds, really is a must on any
itinerary.

Approaching from Pontorson, you will find the River Cues-
non an occasional companion to the left of the road; from
Beauvoir the road virtually skirts the bank. The horizon is
dominated by the soaring masonry of the great Abbey,
surmounted by a nineteenth-century spire with its figure of St
Michael. The official car park is conveniently near.

The Abbey stands on a massive granite outcrop some 80 m
(260 ft) high, rising above the muddy sand flats of La Grève
which stretch out far into the Bay. In the nineteenth century,
when the place was used as a prison, the Grève was an open
sewer at low tide. 'Channelled by brown and stinking rivulets
of slow discharge,' it appalled John Ruskin, 'prepared though
I am to bear this kind of thing in pursuit of the picturesque.'
Fortunately, modern sanitation has abated the nuisance and
one can enjoy the stroll out on to the immense flats for a view
of the Abbey from the seaward side. Go with a guided party.
The sands are treacherous and the tide sweeps in at
tremendous speed.

The entrance through the ramparts circling the base of the
Mount lies across a wooden footbridge and through the Porte

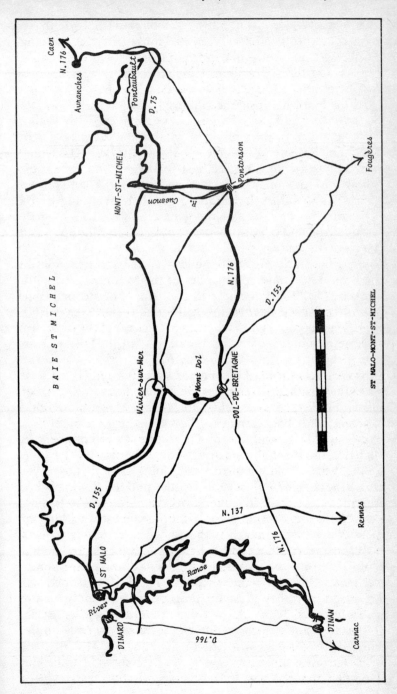

ST MALO-MONT-ST-MICHEL

de l'Avancée. On your left you will find the S.I. in the sixteenth-century citizens' Guard House, for the buildings clustering below the Abbey form the little town of Mont-St-Michel. On the right stands the first town gate, flanked by two fifteenth-century cannon mortars (bombards) captured from the English during the Hundred Years War. Beyond lies the fifteenth-century KING'S GATE, carved with scallop shells (emblem of pilgrims) and salmon, the town's emblem. Through the gate you come on the GRANDE RUE, lined with souvenir shops, bistros, fast-food cafés and restaurants (notably Mère Poulard) and jostling with tourists and pilgrim parties, as it did in the Middle Ages. It is overhung by the projecting upper floors of the gabled houses. Climbing the Grande Rue you pass the Musée Historial du Mont opposite the eleventh-century parish church. An alley to the left leads to the Maison de Tiphaine, built, according to tradition, by the Breton hero and commander of the Mount, Bertrand du Guesclin (1320-80), for his wife Tiphaine. The stepped street now turns sharp left for the Abbey staircase, the GRAND DEGRÉ. On your right is the entrance to the Abbey Gardens and steps mounting to the ramparts' North Tower, from which there is a fine PANORAMA.

Make the full tour of the ramparts after viewing the Abbey. After the North Tower comes the Boucle Tower, the Cholet, Basse, Liberty, Arcade and King's Towers, from which a staircase leads back down to the Grande Rue.

Follow the Grand Degré up to the fourteenth-century Châtelet, the fortified entrance to the Abbey itself. The stairs of the Escalier du Gouffre ('the Gulf') lead to the abbey Guardroom, beyond which is the pillared and vaulted Almonry. The guided tour starts here. It will take you through stone corridors and steep staircases within the mountain of stone which is the Abbey.

According to legend the first church here, an eighth-century oratory chapel, was inspired by a vision of St Michael by the local bishop. In the ninth century it had developed into a substantial abbey. The building of the present structure began in the 1110s. The Carolingian building was used as a crypt and foundations; granite blocks were hauled for miles and then had to be winched to the summit. Much of the structure rests on platforms built out from the side of the hill. Building continued well into the sixteenth century. The route of the tour, as will be seen, follows convenience rather than chronology and the earliest buildings are among the last to be visited.

Yet another climb brings you to the terrace known as 'Gautier's Leap' (from a prisoner said to have committed suicide here) and, passing through a thirteenth-century side portal of the church, to the great WEST PLATFORM, a spacious terrace with stunning PANORAMAS resulting from the demolition of the final two bays of the church's nave. Built in the 1020s and 1030s, it has been much altered (the false floor, for example), nevertheless the powerful Romanesque style of the architecture contrasts with the fine Flamboyant work of the CHANCEL (1450s-1520s). Chapels radiate from the ambulatory. Outside, a magical scaffolding of buttresses, flying buttresses and pinnacles rises to support the chancel.

The monastery cloister which we now come to forms the second storey of one of Europe's greatest Gothic achievements, an architectural complex known as the MERVEILLE ('Marvel'). Built in the 1220s, the CLOISTER is elegant and light, the arcades supported on clustered columns are richly carved and look out over the sea – a breathtaking vista. On the S. side is the lavatorium where the monks washed their hands before entering the REFECTORY: this is magically lit by narrow windows, cunningly concealed from the entrance, and two great end windows. Descending to the crypts we pass the Chapel of St Stephen with, nearby, the housing of the huge wheel used to winch the monks' food up from the kitchens to the Refectory. The fifteenth-century CRYPTE DES GROS PILIERS ('pillars') has five massive pillars, each some 5 m (16 ft) in circumference. The SALLE DES CHEVALIERS ('Knights' Hall'), with its beautiful vaulting, was built as the scriptorium in the thirteenth century; the name was changed in the fifteenth century when King Louis XI founded the chivalric order of St Michael with the Abbey as its home chapel. The adjacent SALLE DES HÔTES ('Guest Hall') (1210s) has two majestic fireplaces and was the scene of the ceremonial receptions for King St Louis IX in the thirteenth century and King Francis I in the sixteenth on their return from pilgrimages. The floor below comprises the storeroom (*cellier*) and the Almonry, where alms were dispensed, and where we began our tour.

RENNES

Route (St Malo): N.137
Distance: 69 km (44 mi)
*Historic capital of Brittany; city shopping; museum; vintage
car collection.*

With a population of some 210,000, two universities and
major electronics and communications industries, Rennes is
one of the first cities of France. A day here can make a
welcome change of pace from the resort atmosphere of old St
Malo and Dinard. And there are some noteworthy tourist
atttractions.

The N.137 brings you in along the R. St Malo and R. St
Martin to a T-junction with the R. Fougères. Car enthusiasts
turn left here for the MUSÉE AUTOMOBILE DE BRE-
TAGNE (closed between noon and 2 p.m.), just 3.5 km (2½
mi) out of town. This major vintage car collection holds some
70 models, all in working order, with an 1899 de Dion-
Bouton among its prized exhibits. Turning right for the town
centre, you pass the old church of St Melaine (also called
Nôtre Dame) with the beautiful Jardin du Thabor park
behind it (botanical and landscape gardens). A right turn at
the canalized River Vilaine will bring you to the Cathedral
area.

The Great Fire of Rennes in 1720 demolished most of the
medieval city. Today, the first impression is of a grid plan of
somewhat austere eighteenth-century granite buildings and
unimpressive modern architecture. However, parts of the old
town survived in the Cathedral area. The nineteenth-century
cathedral church of St Pierre (the third on the site since the
sixth century) has a fine sixteenth-century Flemish altarpiece
in a chapel near the S. transept. Walk round the N. side of the
Cathedral to 3 R. St Guillaume (now a restaurant), a
medieval house possibly owned by Bertrand du Guesclin, the
Breton hero. Cross the Cathedral Square to the MORDE-
LAISE GATE, all that is left of the old ramparts and the
ceremonial entrance used by the medieval dukes of Brittany
on their way to installation in the Cathedral. Continue on to
the Place des Lices, formerly the 'lists' for jousts and tournaments, graced by two fine sixteenth-century mansions. From
here the half-timbered houses lining the R. St Michel are a

fitting prelude to the sixteenth-century buildings of the Place Ste Anne. Leave by the R. de Pont-aux-Foulons, where the old houses accommodate some first-rate modern shops. After the R. and Place du Camp Jacquet, turn left along the R. Lafayette and its continuation to the PALAIS DE JUSTICE.

This seventeenth-century building, formerly the Parlement of Brittany, was designed by Salamon de Brosse (he died during the work). From the spacious pillared entrance hall the grand staircase (1720s) leads to richly decorated rooms of which the Grande Chambre (formerly the Parlement debating chamber) is especially noteworthy. Below the ornamental coffered ceiling, ornate boxes provided seating for the public. The great room (some 20 m, 66 ft long) is embellished with painted and gilded wood carving. Modern Gobelins tapestries lining the walls depict episodes in Breton history. From the SE corner of the Place de Bretagne, the R. St Georges (group of old half-timbered houses) leads to the seventeenth-century Abbaye de St Georges, now municipal offices, and a pleasant public garden. Turn right down the R. Gambetta across the River Vilaine for the PALAIS DES MUSÉES.

The ground-floor houses the Musée de Bretagne. Local history collections depict the history of the province from the Gallo-Roman period to the arrival of the Celtic Britons who fled across the Channel from the fifth- and sixth-century Anglo-Saxon invasions and up to the 1900s. Tableaux and dioramas depict typical scenes from Breton life from the Middle Ages to the nineteenth century. Rural crafts and traditional costumes are well represented and the tour concludes with an audio-visual presentation of contemporary Breton life. It all helps to convey to the visitor the background for the strong sense of local nationalism. The Musée des Beaux-Arts in the upper galleries, one of France's main provincial collections, has masterpieces from the sixteenth to the twentieth century. The emphasis is heavily on French art (fine paintings by Chardin, Corot, Gauguin, etc.) but there are also important works by Veronese, Rubens, Vlaminck and Picasso. In addition there are interesting collections of old master drawings, of Egyptian and classical art, and of porcelain.

Trips from the
CAPITAL

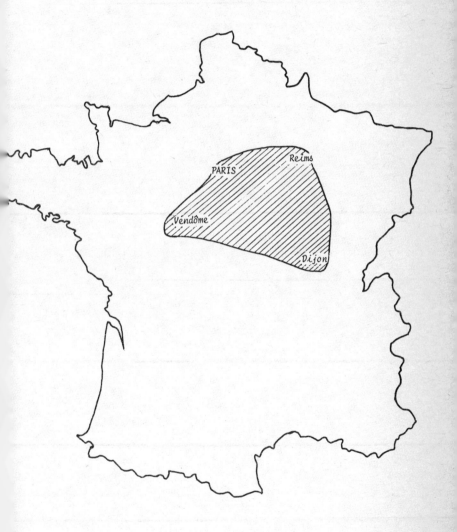

PARIS

Beaune		TGV
Chartres		88 km (55 mi)
Dijon		TGV
Fontainebleau		65 km (40½ mi)
Reims		140 km (88 mi)
Vendôme		178 km (111 mi)
Versailles		22 km (14 mi)
Château Gaillard	*Dieppe	92 km (58 mi)
Giverny	*Dieppe	85 km (53 mi)
Lyon	*Arles	TGV
Rouen	*Dieppe	140 km (87½ mi)

BEAUNE

Route (Paris): TGV to Dijon, then local train
Hospice de Beaune, majestic old alms house; Collegiate Church of Nôtre Dame; Burgundy wine museum.

Since if you visit Beaune at all you are almost certain to return some day you may, on your first visit, make it an excursion from Dijon.

From the station, the Ave 8 Septembre leads to the fortified gate in the fourteenth-century RAMPARTS. Continue along the R. des Tonneliers (coopers) and then left along R. Carno. The Gothic-fronted Hôtel de la Rochepot on the corner is in fact mid-sixteenth-century, as can be seen from its Renaissance-style courtyard. Across the road is the fifteenth-

century belfry of the old town hall. Continue on to the Place
Carnot and from there to the magical HÔTEL-DIEU, the
former HOSPICE DE BEAUNE.

Begun in 1442, it was built at the expense of Nicholas
Rolin, Chancellor to Duke Philip 'the Good' of Burgundy,
whose domains stretched from Burgundy to the Low Countries and who ruled the towns of Flanders such as *Bruges
and *Ghent. The architect of the Hospice was the Fleming
Jehan Wisecrère and the steeply pitched gables and dormers,
crocketed pinnacles and parti-coloured geometric tile patterns recall the architecture of those regions. Set in the rolling
countryside of Burgundy, the building has something of a

fairy-tale aspect and its history is almost as romantic. Endowed as a charitable hospital in the charge of an order of nuns from Malines (Mechlin, Belgium), it continued to fulfil its original function for more than 500 years and today it houses an old people's home. There are frequent guided tours through the great Salle des Malades; the Infirmary (72 m, 235 ft long); the chapel; the kitchen and dispensary (with an interesting collection of old bottles and utensils) and the small gallery housing the Rogier van der Weyden's polyptych, *The Last Judgement*, commissioned for the chapel. Either side of the Christ in Judgement in the central panel can be seen the Duke, the Chancellor and the Chancellor's son with the Virgin and Apostles and the Duchess, the Chancellor's wife and daughter with St John the Baptist and Apostles opposite them. The great picture remained in the chapel until the Revolution, when the hospital itself seemed in danger of dissolution. Today the hospital and its work are financed in part from the annual wine auction of its renowned Hospice de Beaune and Côtes de Beaune wines.

The S.I. opposite the Hôtel Dieu will give you details of the numerous *caves* and *vignerons* which offer *dégustations* (wine tastings). Take the Ave de la République for the collegiate CHURCH OF NÔTRE DAME. Dating mostly from the twelfth and thirteenth centuries, its great treasure is the sequence of superb fifteenth-century TAPESTRIES on the life of the Virgin, also commissioned by Cardinal Jean Rolin, son of the famous chancellor. From the church find the R. de l'Enfer for the old mansion of the dukes of Burgundy which houses an excellent MUSEUM OF WINE; next door is a fourteenth-century wine press house or *cuverie* with some old presses on show.

These are the principal sights of Beaune, apart from the town itself. On a fine summer's day it is a place to explore at leisure. Historic town houses grace the streets; the ramparts invite inspection and the restaurants, from reasonable to expensive, offer generally first-rate food. The small Musée des Beaux-Arts in the Hôtel de Ville in the north of town has a display of chromophotography, a system of colour photography invented here in the early 1900s, and some fine romantic landscapes by the local artist Felix Ziem (d. 1911). However, you might be well advised to head for the railway station after lunch for a long afternoon in *Dijon.

CHARTRES

Route (Paris): A.12/N.10 or A.10/A.11
Distance: 88 km (55 mi)
Cathedral; stained glass, sculptures; view across the fields.

If you are travelling by car consider taking a somewhat longer route than either of the above – the N.12 to Dreux and then the N.154 for Chartres. The distant view from across the fields of the great church rising above the roofs of the town is part of the experience of Chartres. The detour will add more than half an hour to your journey time and the view is much better from the north than from the motorway. But whichever route you choose *and* if you come by train, start your tour at the Cathedral. Chartres has many charms as a town in its own right, but the great church is the reason for your visit.

In 1194 a great fire destroyed the 'new' cathedral begun at Chartres barely 50 years before. The disaster sparked an extraordinary response. Thousands of devout volunteers – noblemen, monks and peasants among them – came from all over France, we are told, to labour on the structure designed to replace it. The result was the CATHEDRAL OF NÔTRE DAME we see today. Many earlier great churches had been conceived as places of pilgrimage, but Chartres, the world's most famous Gothic church, was from the start a place of popular worship. The first burst of building ran from the 1190s to the 1260s.

Earlier structures left their mark. The W. end of the earlier building was incorporated (some mid-twelfth-century sculptures can be seen on the Royal portal), as was an older crypt at the eastern end. Elements of the earlier Romanesque style survive in the rounded arches and the sturdily beautiful buttresses which surround the exterior and in the steeple on the right tower of the W. front. Despite the initial enthusiasm, the building was not completed on its original plan. The elaborate left tower dates from the 1500s.

Compared with, say, Reims, the W. front at Chartres is almost stark. But the lithe and vigorous sculptures of the famous Royal Portal are quite superb. Above the central door is Christ in Majesty, to its right the Nativity and to the left the Ascension. Within, the church is full of drama. The pillars

soaring to the Gothic vaulting are sensed in the glowing gloom of the stunning thirteenth-century glass. Dominated by lustrous reds and blues, the colour scheme is deeply rich. It is rare to find a medieval church with so much of its original glass intact (less than 10 per cent of the 8,000 sq m/26,000 square feet is replacement, and there is even some twelfth-century work from the earlier church). Browse past the unfolding episodes of biblical stories, saints and prophets and notice how the leads which hold the fragments of coloured glass in place were used by the master glaziers to give vitality and diversity to their designs. The great rose windows in the W. end and the N. portal are truly grand conceptions. Do not leave the church before you have inspected the ancient crypt (guided tours only), the Cathedral TREASURY and the side portals.

The MUSÉE DES BEAUX-ARTS, to the N. of the Cathedral gardens, is housed in the former episcopal palace. Among its treasures are some fine enamels, e.g. a thirteenth-century processional cross, and a comprehensive collection of paintings. Notable are a sixteenth-century portrait of Erasmus by Hans Holbein and some fine twentieth-century works by Vlaminck and others.

S. of the Cathedral stand some attractive old houses, among them 35 R. des Ecuyers, with an intriguing carved staircase. Continue along the R. St Pierre to the magnificent CHURCH OF ST PIERRE. Begun in the twelfth century (the massive tower and the apse date from this period), it has glass and buttressing which almost rival the glories of the Cathedral. From here you may cross the river and stroll up to the R. Porte Guillaume for a view of the old walls.

DIJON

Route (Paris): TGV, Gare de Lyon, depart 8.05 (check time)
Journey time: approx. 1 hr 40 mins
Cathedral of St Bénigne; Palais des Ducs; Musée des Beaux-Arts; Church of Nôtre Dame; medieval-Renaissance mansions.

Start your tour of the CATHEDRAL OF ST BÉNIGNE in the crypt, all that remains of a Romanesque church of the early 1000s. The great circular space with its ambulatory is reminiscent of Jerusalem's Church of the Holy Sepulchre. Today the most lasting impression is made by the hauntingly primitive figure carvings on the capitals – more suited to the imagined rites of the Druidical sacred grove than to a Christian sanctuary. The strong, simple lines of the architecture itself (some of which dates back to a still earlier, ninth-century structure) is deeply impressive. The church is mostly thirteenth-century.

N. of the church is the MUSÉE ARCHÉOLOGIQUE. Its principal treasure is the bust of Christ by the Dutch sculptor Claus Sluter (d. 1406). Originally part of his Well of Moses at the Chartreuse of Champmol (see below), it reveals an artist with an expressive power that anticipates Michelangelo. Other pieces include sculptures, bronze statuettes and arte-facts from the Gallo-Roman period. S. of the Cathedral in the R. Michelet stands the twelfth-century church of St Philibert. Continue on to the Place Bossuet and the R. Piron and R. Amiral, left up the R. Vauban with its handsome old mansions (notably nos. 21 and 12) to the Place de la Libération. Here a decision is needed. Facing you is the Hôtel de Ville and (to the right) the Musée des Beaux-Arts on the site of the former Palais des Ducs. In the R. des Bons Enfants (leading off to the right), a seventeenth-century mansion houses the Musée Magnin. Named after the nineteenth-century art collector who lived here, it has a lovely courtyard and a delightful series of rooms with fine furniture and some good paintings. A sumptuous experience, it may nevertheless have to be passed up since no one who visits Dijon should miss the complex known as the PALAIS DES DUCS.

One of the few parts of the original medieval structure to survive is the Tour Philippe le Bon, approached from the Cour d'Honneur opposite the Place de la Libération (magnificent views of Dijon and the mountains and wine country round about). For the MUSÉE DES BEAUX-ARTS go through the Palace complex to the Place des Ducs de Bourgogne and round the corner of the building. One of the richest provincial collections in Europe, the museum holds paintings from all the major European schools from the fourteenth to the nineteenth centuries. German and Flemish works are particularly well represented. There are also good collections of porcelain, arms and armour and twentieth-century art. But the glories of the place are the monumental tombs of Dukes Philip the Bold ('*Le Hardie*') and John the Fearless ('*Sans Peur*') in the SALLE DES GARDES, the guardroom of the fifteenth-century ducal palace. For these and the ducal kitchens (1440s) and the medieval Salle de la Ste Chapelle, follow the layout plans displayed. The great TOMBS, originally in the Chartreuse de Champmol, were dismantled at the time of the Revolution but reassembled here in the 1820s. Life-size effigies rest on black marble slabs, supported by white marble arcading which stands on stepped black marble plinths. The monument to Philip the Bold (d. 1404) befits the founder of the Burgundian state. Two kneeling angels, with gilded hair and wings, support his helmet, his head rests on a cushion of painted red (velvet), he wears a blue cape, tasselled with gold, and a ducal coronet; a lion with gilded mane crouches at his feet. The ornately carved Gothic arcading beneath is peopled with a mourners' procession of some 40 cowled monks and courtiers. Sluter worked on the monument from 1384: it was completed by Claus Werve. The other tomb, of Duke John and his wife, is still more ornate. Commissioned by their son Duke Philip the Good in the 1440s from the Aragonese sculptor Juan de la Huerta it follows the model of the earlier work but here we have four angels and two lions and the vivid blue of the duchess's gown. On the walls of the guardroom hang rich tapestries, and altarpieces, and a portrait of Philip the Good. At the end of the room there is a massive, ornate chimneypiece. The whole room makes a grand testimony to the golden age of the Burgundian state.

From the Museum take the little street across the Place des Ducs de Bourgogne to the R. de la Chouette for the seventeenth-century Hôtel de Vogue at no. 8. Turn right here for some of the best streets of old Dijon. To your left is the dramatic thirteenth-century CHURCH OF NÔTRE DAME. The façade is a riot of human and grotesque animal heads, and one of the turrets supports the Jacquemart clock, plundered by Duke Philip the Bold from Courtrai after his victory there over the towns of Flanders in 1382. The blacksmith who strikes the hours is original; in the early 1600s the Dijonnais presented him with a wife, and the son and daughter followed in subsequent centuries. The Hôtel Bouhier de Lantenay at 40 R. de la Préfecture is worth a detour but do not miss the R. des Forges (a pedestrian precinct by the Hôtel de Ville). The fifteenth-century Hôtels Chambellan (housing the S.I.) and Morel Sauvgrain are perhaps most distinguished of many splendid mansions. Beyond stand the half-timbered houses of the Place François Rude and two streets N. of that is the OPEN MARKET (Tuesdays, Fridays and Saturdays). From here follow the R. de la Liberté (home of Grey Poupon, the famous Dijon mustard) to the Place Darcy and so to the station.

[For centuries, the glory of Dijon was the CHARTREUSE DE CHAMPMOL, endowed by Duke Philip the Bold. One of many of France's religious monuments destroyed during the Revolution, today it is little more than a site: only the portal of the abbey church and the wellhead of the main courtyard survive. Both are adorned by sculptures by Claus Sluter which make the site, 1 km (½ mi) beyond the station along the Ave Albert 1er, a place of pilgrimage for art-lovers. The Virgin and Child form the centrepiece of the portal; to their right stand the figures of the Duke and St John the Baptist, to their right those of the Duchess and St Catherine. The Well of Moses (PUITS DE MOÏSE) is one of the masterpieces of Western sculpture. King David, Moses and four prophets stand at the six faces of the hexagonal wellhead. In each figure Sluter achieves an insight into character and a vigour of line in the draperies never approached before and rarely equalled since.]

FONTAINEBLEAU

Route (Paris): N.7 or A.6/N.7
Distance: 60 km (37½ mi)
Château and Forêt de Fontainebleau; Barbizon village.

The N.7 brings you in on the R. de France to Place Napoléon
(S.I.).

The name Fontainebleau, from medieval Latin 'Fons
Bliaudi', 'the Spring of Bliaud', may recall some legendary,
possibly Celtic, prince but the place has been associated with
the French monarchy at least since the twelfth century. Set in
the still extensive and beautiful FORÊT DE FONTAINE-
BLEAU it was the site of a royal hunting lodge in the early
twelfth century. In the 1160s King Louis VII built a chapel
(consecrated by St Thomas à Becket, in exile from England)
and his grandson, King St Louis IX, made further additions
of which the tower in the Oval Court survives. Thereafter,
the place suffered something of decline until 1528 when King
Francis I began building the magnificent royal residence we
see today. Hoping perhaps to bathe in reflected antique glory

Napoleon, self-crowned 'Emperor' of France, preferred it to Versailles, calling it 'the house of centuries'.

From the Place Napoléon Bonaparte follow the R. Denecourt round to the Place Général de Gaulle and so to the handsome wrought-iron gates of the Cours 'des Adieux', formerly 'du Cheval Blanc' ('White Horse' Court). The gates are gilded with Napoleon's monogram and the eagles of empire; it was here that he made his adieus to his soldiers when he went into his first exile on the Isle of Elba. A drive of stone sets leads through formal lawns to the central range of Francis I's palace, designed in Italianate Renaissance style by the architect Giles le Breton. The sweeping horseshoe staircase to the first-floor entrance, somewhat out of proportion to the façade, was added in the seventeenth century. Left of the entrance is the chapel; to the right are the Queen Mother's Apartments, among which the Galerie des Assiettes is decorated with plates of Sèvres porcelain. Opposite the main entrance is the GALERIE FRANÇOIS 1er. Reckoned to be one of Europe's finest interiors, the decorative scheme conceived by the Florentine painter Il Rosso took ten years to complete. Deep wainscotting of carved walnut, with emblems of power and the gilded monogram 'F', runs the length of the walls; above it painted panels and stucco reliefs depict the allegorical subjects beloved of Renaissance scholarship. Beams support a wooden coffered ceiling of lozenges and triangles. In 1541 Il Rosso was succeeded by Primaticcio. With other Italians including Niccolò dell'Abbate they formed a 'School of Fontainebleau' which exerted a deep influence on the course of French art.

From the great gallery the Guardroom leads, via the mid-1700s Royal Staircase, to the magnificent Ballroom (by the architect Philibert de l'Orme) with the interlaced monograms 'H' and 'D' (for Henry II and his mistress Diane de Poitiers) and mythological paintings by Primaticcio and dell'Abbate. Returning to the Guardroom, you pass through a room in the thirteenth-century Tour de St Louis to the ROYAL APARTMENTS of the Oval Court. From these the Council Chamber (paintings by Boucher and van Loo) brings you to the Apartments of Napoleon. Below are the PETITS APPARTEMENTS occupied by Napoleon and Josephine, with Louis XV and Louis XVI decor and Empire-style furniture.

In the grounds the Fontaine Bliaud stands in the English Garden while across the way lies the great Carp Pond with its lovely island pavilion. Through the Fountain Court and the parterre formal gardens you come to the Cascade with the Grand Canal, now divided from it by a road, stretching away into the distance. Returning through the Parterre, cross the Oval Court (note the Tour de St Louis) and skirt the Cours des Offices to the Garden of Diana before leaving the Palace precincts.

Other sights in Fontainebleau include the Napoleonic Museum, R. St Honoré. If you are planning to tour the Forest a trip to the village of BARBIZON, about 9 km (5½ mi) away, is worth considering. Take the N.837 for Milly and watch for signposts. In the mid-nineteenth century a group of artists, headed by Theodore Rousseau and Millet, worked from here, devoting themselves to simple landscapes and peasant scenes, '*paysages intimes*', and working directly from nature. Inspired in part by John Constable they were forerunners of the Impressionists in '*plein air*', i.e. out-of-doors, painting. It is still a popular, even fashionable, haunt for painters.

Another delightful little trip in the forest is to Moret-sur-Loing (N.6 for Sens, 6.5 km, 4 mi) with its medieval fortifications and memories of the Impressionist painters Pissarro and Alfred Sisley.

From 1941 to August 1944 Fontainebleau was German military HQ and thenceforward, for some years, that of the Allied forces in Europe.

REIMS

Route (Paris): A.4, but leave the autoroute at the exit for the N.31 on the outskirts of Reims
Distance: 140 km (88 mi)
Cathedral; Musée des Beaux-Arts; champagne caves.

The N.31 will bring you in along the Ave de Paris/R. Fabien/R. de Vesle. At the R. des Capuchins (fourth right after the river) turn right and then left for the R. Jadart with the S.I. Nearby is the Musée des Beaux-Arts and a little beyond that the CATHEDRAL.

Capital of the Celtic Remi, the city was an important Roman centre and converted to Christianity in the third century. It was here, in 496, that St Remigius crowned Clovis king of the Franks in the first cathedral. Thenceforward, Reims was to be the coronation city of France and the chrism and regalia held here the only authentic emblems of kingship. In 1429 Charles VII, whose legitimacy was denied by his own mother and whose right to the crown was challenged by Henry VI of England, was crowned with Joan of Arc holding the banner. The coronation established Charles's claims beyond question (many French had supported Henry) and Henry's coronation in Nôtre Dame, Paris, shortly after was a hollow charade. During World War I most of the city was demolished in heavy German bombardments. The devastation during World War II was almost as great but it was at General Eisenhower's GHQ here on 7 May 1945 that the German unconditional surrender was signed.

The CATHEDRAL, culmination of French Gothic architecture, is remarkable not only for its beauty but also for the comparative speed of its building, *c.* 1210-50. Many of Europe's great medieval churches (*Chartres, for example) were left incomplete for centuries and their original plans abandoned. But at Reims the cruciform plan, the great height of the nave, the rise of the multiple piers and clustered columns through triforium and clerestory, the vast area of window space and the profuse series of sculptures adorning the exterior – all were done as planned. The overall effect is of compelling unity. Some changes there were: rose windows replaced the original, more conventional, scheme of carved tympana over the front portals while some of the statues done in the 1220s for the W. front were moved to the 'Judgement' and St Sixtus porches on the N. side.

The W. front, 88 m (267 ft) to the top of the towers and with its great rose window, 13 m (40 ft) in diameter, is stunning. Like Nôtre Dame, Paris, it has three horizontal stages, but whereas at Paris the divisions are strongly marked, here they merge into an overall design. The sculptural programme around and above the portals is echoed by the line of saints and kings in the top stage.

Although vandalized and mutilated during the Revolution, the W. front sculptures still tell their story. Above the deeply recessed central portal are scenes in the life of the Virgin; to the right is Christ in Judgement and to the left the Crucifixion (the head of the famous 'Smiling Angel', the *Sourire de Reims*', is restored). Just below the towers, a line of colossal statues of the kings of France has the baptism of Clovis as the centrepiece. On the N. side notice the Porte de l'Enfer and the triple portal with statues originally on the W. front.

Inside, the glorious rose window can be more fully appreciated; it is surrounded by yet more superb examples of high Gothic sculpture, both dramatic and realistic. The S. façade of the Cathedral was severely damaged during World War I; little of the original glass remains and parts of it were replaced as best as possible in new locations. There is a Chagall window (1974) in the Lady Chapel, which also contains a number of mid-sixteenth-century Flemish tapestries. Do not leave this great church without walking round the outside, where the pinnacles and flying buttresses build up a massive and coherent 'sculpture' in their own right.

S. of the Cathedral the Palais du Tau, formerly the archbishop's palace, houses a museum containing religious relics, pieces of statuary and tapestries from the fifteenth to the nineteenth centuries. W. of the Cathedral (near the S.I.) is the MUSÉE DES BEAUX-ARTS (Musée de St Denis). Among its treasures are a series of portrait drawings by the German artist Lucas Cranach (1462-1553); paintings by the Le Nain brothers; works by Philippe de Champagne and also Boucher; and works by the major French artists from Delacroix to Matisse.

N. of the Cathedral the Place Royale is on the site of the Roman forum, where fragments of stonework can be seen, while a little further N. the museum of Old Reims in the

Hôtel le Vergeur has collections of furniture and ceramics and reconstructed sections of old buildings. Continuing northwards beyond the Hôtel de Ville you come to a Roman triumphal arch, the PORTE DE MARS. Turn right along the Boulevard du Champs de Mars for the house of Mumm, the famous CHAMPAGNE company, which offers guided tours of its cellars.

It was not until the late seventeenth century that the first sparkling wines of Champagne were produced. But for centuries the district was considered one of the finest wine regions of France (Henry VIII of England had a vineyard here). It is said that St Remigius, who also owned a vineyard, presented Clovis with a cask of the wine on his christening. Fittingly, the large abbey church of St Rémi in the S. of the city is within easy walking distance of Veuve Clicquot-Ponsardin, Pomméry, Taittinger and Piper-Heidsieck. Like Mumm, all offer guided tours (details from the S.I.). According to tradition it was Dom Pérignon, the cellarer of the Benedictine abbey of Hautvilliers between Ay and Épernay, who developed the first *méthode champenois*. Devotees of the wine may well wish to extend their trip to Reims with a visit to Épernay.

VENDÔME

Route (Paris): A.10/A.11 to interchange S. of Chartres, then N.10 via Châteaudun (worth stopping)
Distance: 178 km (111 mi)
Castle; Trinity Church; picturesque riverside walks; markets.

A real break from the capital in one of France's typically charming provincial towns. Modestly good local wines, mushrooms and goat cheeses are specialities. This is a place to discover.

You drive through the outskirts to the River Loir. Turn right along the Mail du Maréchal Leclerc; the second turn left, R. des États-Unis, takes you over the river and then a small branch of it to a T-junction for another left turn, which brings you at length to the castle mound, where there is parking.

The ancient Celtic settlement here became a Roman centre of some importance. Then, in the eleventh century, the lords of the place, the Counts of Anjou, built the CASTLE and founded the abbey of La Trinité (see below). Today, the ruined battlements on the castle hill, dominated by the Tour de Poitiers, enclose a pleasant lawned park with a good view of the town below.

From the castle, the R. Ferme leads to the main road, where you turn right (past the old half-timbered guildhall of the masons) to cross the river and enter the town by the PORTE ST GEORGES. Almost a fairy-tale ideal of what a town gate should be, with its steep, tiled roofs and massive circular flanking towers, it was built in the fourteenth century but reworked in the sixteenth. Ahead stretches the R. Poterie.

Immediately on your right the Quai St Georges hairpins back, skirting pleasant lawns and town houses to the river, and then to the renovated COVERED MARKET, the glass walls of which shimmer with reflections of the surrounding wooded slopes outside the town. Down to the right runs the R. Guesnault; at the Renaissance-style stone archway of no. 5 pause to peep at the charming courtyard house, described in his novel *La Grande Breteche* by Balzac, who was a schoolboy in Vendôme. Return to the R. Poterie by the R. Saulnerie, where you turn right for the next crossroads. Here, the left branch takes you to the pretty little twelfth-century Church of St Pierre la Motte, the right to R. Général de Gaulle, a handsome, tree-shaded boulevard on which may be found the town's principal café, and leading to the TOUR ST MARTIN. This late fifteenth-century belfry tower is all that now remains of the former parish church whose site is now occupied by the lovely Place St Martin, behind. (On the N. side stands a splendid fifteenth-century timber-framed house with fascinating old carvings.)

The R. de l'Abbaye leads to the truly magnificent early-1500s Flamboyant W. front of the Church of LA TRINITÉ. Right of it stands the detached BELFRY, with its stone spire (*c.* 1140), rising almost 80 m (260 ft). The swirling lines of the church's window tracery, fretted gable, pinnacles and buttress ornaments are a classic achievement of the 'flame'-like Flamboyant style. The lofty interior is impressive (parts of the original eleventh-century structure are thought to survive in the transept), and the Renaissance wood screen repays attention. The splendid fifteenth-century choir stalls have richly carved bench ends and a series of misericord carvings of the highest quality depicting musicians, fabulous beasts and scenes of everyday life such as treading the grapes.

The canopies above are equally fine. There is good medieval stained glass, but the whole interior has a sadly neglected air. The lanes round the church provide a chance to admire the wonderful buttressing and window lights and also to do some detective work, sorting out remnants of old stonework and timbered structures which may once have belonged to the old abbey buildings, from the backs of modern shops, houses and restaurants in the nearby street. Behind the church you will find a pretty little eleventh-century chapel and the sixteenth-century Priory, while to the S. is a complex of buildings, formerly part of the abbey and now housing local government offices and the MUSEUM. It has extensive collections of local archaeology and history and natural history as well as some attractive paintings.

From the abbey gardens there is an attractive view of the river and the old watergate or Arche des Grands Prés, a curious group of a tower and stone bridge with machicolations spanning a picturesque arm of the river. Returning to the Place Martin, turn right down the R. du Change (pedestrian precinct for much of its length), with a pleasant warren of old streets behind it on the right and unexpected vistas where it crosses the stream on which stands the watergate. From the bridge, where it crosses the main branch of the Loir, you can just see the Tour de l'Islette, the last vestige of the medieval ramparts. On the left a wooden walkway leads you on a delightful stroll across the waterways and through gravelled precincts behind the Hôtel de Ville, the local history museum on the site of the birthplace of Ronsard the poet (1524-85), and to the fifteenth-century château-like Hôtel du Saillant (S.I.). From here you come to the precincts of the Lycée Ronsard (built in 1639 by Duc César de Vendôme, an illegitimate son of King Henry IV whose parents lived in the castle here). It was here that Balzac went to school (school report: 'of good conduct, happy disposition, but rather slow'). The school is built on the site of former Hôpital St Jacques, the chapel still survives, and the R. St Jacques (note the bust on the house of Ronsard's birthplace) leads to the charming Place de la Madeleine (market on Fridays) (good sixteenth-century glass in the church, if open). From here, you can walk the length of the R. Poterie, with glimpses down some of the streets you have already visited, to fix the memory of this delightful town in your mind.

VERSAILLES

Route (Paris): A.13
Distance: 22 km (14 mi)
Rail: Gare des Invalides, Paris (regular services)

Versailles is a large town with a cathedral, museums and other sights worth a visit. There are also some fine restaurants. However, this is a day-trip and the great PALACE, seat of the royal government of Louis XIV from 1682, will fully occupy your time (though it should be said that some people reckon it possible to 'do' Versailles *and* Chartres in one day). The town does contain one other monument more important, perhaps, in the history of modern France than the Palace. This is the Jeu de Paume, the famous tennis court where on 20 June 1789 the deputies of the Tiers État (the Commons) swore the historic oath not to be dismissed without their own consent and to constitute themselves the effective National Assembly. By this act, it was said, the initiative passed finally from the monarch to the assembly. This, even more than the storming of the Bastille in Paris on 14 July, may be said to have marked the beginning of the Revolution. The tennis court itself still stands off the Ave des Sceaux near the Gare Rive Gauche, terminus for the Invalides line.

Inspired, perhaps, by Louis XIV's visit to the palace of Vaux le Vicomte built by his father's minister Fouquet, Versailles was begun in the late 1660s. Fouquet's ostentation was his undoing – he was disgraced, his palace confiscated and his architect, Le Vau, his landscape gardener, Le Nôtre, and his painter, Le Brun, all taken into royal service.

In an age when grandeur meant prestige and prestige meant power, Louis XIV saw the arts as a branch of royal propaganda. The heavy pomp of Versailles was its ultimate expression. In 1662 Louis had his chief minister take over the Paris tapestry works of Gobelins to provide the decor for the new palace. The 'Royal Furnishing Factory' of Gobelins, placed under the artistic direction of Le Brun, produced not only its famous tapestries but furniture, works in gold and silver, statuary, architectural details and even carriages. The style was not over-imaginative but it was impressive and the work was technically excellent and ostentatiously costly.

The first château at Versailles, built by Louis's father King Louis XIII in the 1620s, was used as a hunting lodge. Indeed, apart from the game in the surrounding forests there was little to commend the site. A later courtier called it 'the saddest of places, without a view, without woods and without water'; others called Louis XIV's grand design 'a favourite without merit'. The terrain was a mixture of unstable sandy soils and marshlands and the air was notoriously unhealthy. Thousands of workmen died of marsh fever while the work was in progress and the bodies were taken off by the cartload at night so as not to scare new recruits. Louis's finance minister Colbert protested against the absurd expense; his landscape architect Le Nôtre had to lay drainage channels, feeder canals, pipes, aqueducts and cisterns in a system totalling almost 100 miles in length to supply the vast water gardens and fountains – yet even then they only played to their full height when the King himself was walking the grounds. For all this, the favourite without merit became the most envied and imitated building in Europe.

The immense forecourt is divided between the Cour Royale and, beyond, the Cour de Marbre ('Marble Court'), the oldest part of the palace. In the entrance vestibule, the information office has plans of palace and grounds and details of opening times of the Trianon palaces and of the guided tours to some of the suites of rooms. Indicated below are the principal sights that lie ahead of you, but it is a long trek and you may decide to miss some of the possibilities.

The STATE APARTMENTS are open to the public without guides. First you come to the Chapel, completed only in the 1710s; beyond it lie the Salles du 17e Siècle, with numerous paintings, some of them of Versailles in its early days. On the first floor the Salon d'Hercule forms the ante-room to the state apartments proper. Here the Swiss guards monitored visitors and sightseers. The Salon de Mars is hung with tapestries, designed by Le Brun, depicting Louis XIV's exploits in heroic dimension. You pass through the Salon de Guerre for the renowned Salle des Glaces, the HALL OF MIRRORS. Some 73 m (240 ft) long, it has 17 lofty windows on its garden frontage matched by as many mirrors between marble pilasters, a marble floor and barrel vault with paintings by Le Brun. Among many historic occasions, the Hall of Mirrors witnessed the 1871 treaty which ended the Franco-German war, the proclamation of William I of Prussia as the first Emperor of a united German Empire, and also the signing of the Treaty of Versailles in January 1919 which marked the end of World War I. Next you come to the Cabinet de Conseil, the 1750s Louis XV-style council chamber, and then the King's Bedchamber. This was a focus of the King's almost unbelievably public life – the morning *levée* reception, when he rose from his bed, his meals and his retiring to bed at night, were all public functions watched by scores of people. Louis XV ordered a suite of rooms off the Cabinet de Conseil as a retreat from this kind of public life. The Queen's Bedchamber was the scene of many royal confinements, which were also attended by numerous official witnesses.

Many of the rooms retain their original decor, much of it restored. The Louis Quatorze style was going out of fashion long before the King's death in 1715. The impressive palace was considered inconvenient and uncomfortable. During the winter, the King's mistress complained, the wine froze in its carafes on the tables. During the first year of Louis's great grandson and successor the infant Louis XV, the court gratefully abandoned Versailles for a time. During the regency a lighter, more domestic style became fashionable. Known as rococo, it received its official recognition at court with Louis XV's private apartments and was especially favoured by the royal mistress (1745-64) Mme de Pompadour (her apartments were in the cramped upper floors of the Attiques de Chimay and du Midi).

The vast palace housed hundreds of permanent and semi-permanent residents – the royal family, courtiers and officials, all with their servants, state guests and so forth. Emerging into the grounds, walk down the formal Parterre d'Eau (water-garden) and turn to survey the immense structure – the central block by Le Vau, the wings by his successor Jules Hardouin-Mansart. The low-pitched roofs combined with the quarter-mile length of the range, and the repeating classical details of the windows create what has been called the 'regal monotony of the park front of Versailles'. Le Vau achieved a far more exciting effect in the ORANGERIE to the S. of the Parterre d'Eau, with dignified Doric columns making an elegant contrast to the simple vaulting. Away to the N. of the Parterre d'Eau can be seen the Neptune Basin.

To the west the '*Tapis Vert*' grassed walk leads to the dramatic Apollo Fountain, beyond which the 60-m (200-ft)-wide Grand Canal stretches for a mile into the distance. In its heyday the scene of brilliant boating parties, it sported pleasure craft of all sorts, a replica galley and Venetian gondola complete with Venetian gondoliers among them. The Petit Canal crosses it and leads (N.) towards the GRAND TRIANON Palace (named after the village demolished before its construction in 1687). Built as a retreat for the King, it was also used by Napoleon during his residence at Versailles and contains a good deal of Empire furniture. The walk from the Apollo Fountain through the wooded grounds takes about half an hour. From here you can take the Allée de Trianon back to the main palace (via the Neptune Basin) or explore further towards the PETIT TRIANON (1750s-60s). Alternatively, make more directly for the Petit Trianon along the Allée des Matelots (St Antoine). Built for Louis XV and his mistresses, it was also a favourite haunt of Louis XVI's queen, Marie-Antoinette. Between the two Trianons is a fascinating carriage museum (Musée des Voitures). Beyond the Petit Trianon a walk through the woods takes you past the delightful TEMPLE OF LOVE, 12 Corinthian columns supporting a delicate cupola that shelters the statue of a nymph, to the rustic HAMEAU (hamlet). Here, in idealized country village surroundings, Marie-Antoinette and her ladies played at the peasant life in the fashion for arcadian simplicity inspired (ironically) in part by the writings of Jean-Jacques Rousseau, whose book *Du Contrat Social* was a bible for the Revolutionaries.

Trips from the
DORDOGNE

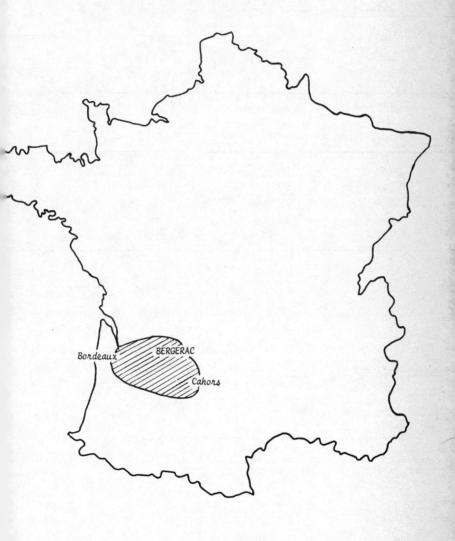

BERGERAC

Bastides tour	145 km (91 mi)
Bordeaux	87 km (53 mi)
Cahors	107 km (67 mi)
St Émilion	56 km (35 mi)

Situated on a broad sweep of the River Dordogne, Bergerac has for centuries been an important centre of the wine trade. From the 1180s to the early 1400s it owed allegiance to the English administration in Bordeaux; during the sixteenth century it was a stronghold of Protestantism.

Today, when the wines of the region are becoming increasingly well known on the British market, the town, with the vineyards which surround it, makes a natural base for a holiday in the Dordogne region. Thanks to restoration work and, it must be said, a certain degree of prettification, the winding streets of the old town overlooking the river frontage offer some attractive and interesting walks – note the vaulted cellars of the old convent, the Cloître des Recollets. There are a few good restaurants, a pleasantly relaxed atmosphere and easy parking in the Places de la Résistance and de la République. There are regular art exhibitions in the seventeenth-century Moulin des Cordeliers while the Hôtel de Ville on the R. Neuve d'Argenson houses the local history museum and France's Museum of Tobacco. There is a boating club on the Promenade Pierre Loti where canoes, etc., can be hired; also here are a clay pigeon shoot and an airport, with its own aero club and centre for parachuting.

There are a number of good restaurants in the countryside round Bergerac (though beware: some are closed for lunch and open only for the evening meal). About 7 km (4½ mi) out of town the splendid sixteenth-century Château de Monbazillac serves a very decent lunch. Famed for its liquorous sweet wines, the castle looks out from its hill over a panorama of vineyards. Although the portcullis gives it a somewhat military air, the spreading lawns, the conical tower roofs and climbing dormer windows remind one of the grander châteaux of the Loire. Barely a mile away, along winding roads between the fields, is the Château la Borderie-Nailhac, a friendly family concern producing wines to match or even outdo those of the main château. There are of course scores of other *vignerons* in the neighbourhood who offer *dégustations*.

A TOUR OF THE BASTIDES

Distance: 145 km (91 mi) (see sketch map)

This day-trip through history offers some surprises. The '*bastides*', to be found all over this part of France, are new towns built some 700 years ago, by French noblemen and English kings, for a variety of economic, political and administrative reasons. The thirteenth-century was a time of great economic expansion. New towns encouraged trade with their markets, offered safe havens in this heavily wooded terrain (at a time when forests were refuges for bandits and outlaws), and also provided bases for local administration. Occasionally they also provided military strongholds. Some of the *bastides* are equipped with defensive walls and ramparts. In many cases these defences, although promised at the founding of the new town, remained unbuilt. There are numerous appeals in the Public Record Office in London from Gascon *bastides* begging the king to build the walls – as protection from the bandits in the surrounding forests. It seems that outlaws were a greater problem than the armies of the French king.

The tour lies through classic Dordogne landscapes and will take you to some of the most fascinating country towns in France, with the rather unexpected feature that many of the marketplaces you will be visiting received their first charters from the chancery in London.

LALINDE, the first on the route, is laid out on the grid plan to be found in many medieval new towns. The most logical layout for a new town, it was in use long before the building of New York. Relics of the English foundation are to be seen in a street two blocks W. off the little marketplace, where a

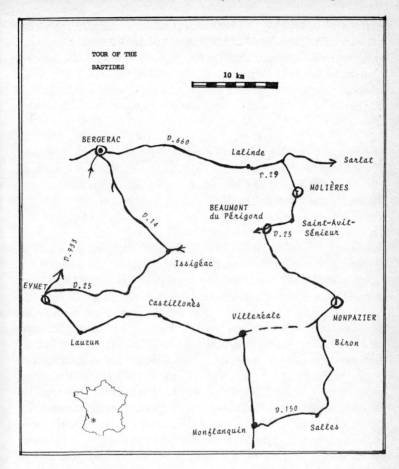

TOUR OF THE
BASTIDES

10 km

BERGERAC   *D.660*   *Lalinde*   → *Sarlat*
P.29
MOLIÈRES
D.14   BEAUMONT
du Périgord
Saint-Avit-
D.25   Sénieur
D.933
Issigéac
EYMET   *D.25*
Castillonès
Villeréale   MONPAZIER
Lauzun   Biron
D.150
Monflanquin   Salles

fine old town gate still stands. Leaving the car in the marketplace, walk down to the river to see parts of the medieval stone harbour defences.

Cross the river and follow the D.25 to the isolated little hilltop *bastide* of MOLIÈRES. At the top of the town is an open grassy square surrounded by old houses and sections of wide-arched arcading supporting first-floor rooms. Today the arcades are used by the house-owners as carports. When the place was built such arcades, or '*cornières*', surrounded the whole square and framed a busy marketplace. Before leaving Molières look into the church where there is a charming little statue of St Joan of Arc, clad in armour and carrying her banner. From the fact that copies are to be found in other churches hereabouts it seems obvious that the model was a standard line of some commercial image-maker.

Continue along the D.25 for St Avit Senieur, a forbidding fortress church, and then on to BEAUMONT DU PÉRIGORD. Now you can get some idea of the *bastides* in their heyday. The main road brings you past impressive old houses and a sturdy old church with a belfry and then into the marketplace, where the *cornières* are complete and crowded of a morning with a typical French open market – though one in this case whose charter goes back to Edward I of England and the year 1297. Beaumont is one of those *bastides* where the walls *were* built, and if you take the little street from the corner of the marketplace opposite the main road you can see one of the old town gates.

Leave by the D.660 for MONPAZIER. Justly renowned as the finest of the *bastides* of the region, it has a fine old timber market hall (usually with the medieval grain measures on display) surrounded by the wide, low-pointed arches of the classic *cornières*. During the market, the honey-stone arcades will be cluttered with crates and Citroën or Renault vans, café tables and, of course, people. Come the afternoon and all will be calm and sun-washed like a stage set waiting for a pageant. In fact, late in August you may well find it hung with banners and shields, since Monpazier sometimes mounts tournament festivals in conjunction with the nearby castle of BIRON. This dramatic hill-top fortress comes next on your itinerary. Built in the thirteenth century, it is being lovingly restored by the *Département* authorities. The result is a splendid castle, which also, incidentally, commands a superb view of the surrounding countryside.

Now through Gavaudun and Salles for the D.150 for MONFLANQUIN. An anti-climax after Monpazier, it is nevertheless a pretty place.

Next, on to VILLERÉALE with its interesting market hall and church and so to CASTILLONÈS. Founded by Alphonse de Poitiers in 1259, it retains traces of its *cornières* and of the fourteenth-century ramparts and town gates. The Château at Lauzun is worth a visit, but be sure to leave time to enjoy the glories of EYMET, 7 km (4 mi) on along the D.111. Founded in the thirteenth century, this beautiful riverside market town has retained its ancient arcades and buildings virtually intact. The narrow streets, lined with stone and timber-framed houses from the fifteenth and sixteenth centuries, offer glimpsed views of the tree-lined river banks and beg to be explored. Complete with a fine château, locally renowned young wines and a reputation for its conserves and confectionery, Eymet is a place to relish. Returning to Bergerac along the D.25/D.14/N.21, you pass through the pretty, medieval episcopal town of Issigéac.

BORDEAUX

Route (Bergerac): D.936
Distance: 87 km (53 mi)
Fine eighteenth-century town planning; memories of English medieval Bordeaux – Cathedral of St André, Pey Berland tower; Musée des Beaux-Arts; Museum of the Resistance.

Approaching along the D.936 you cross first the River Dordogne and then the Garonne, which flow together into the great Gironde estuary a few miles to the north. Although 98 km (60 mi) from the sea, Bordeaux is a major port and has a large industrial zone. Crossing the nineteenth-century Pont de Pierre over the Garonne, you see the Tour St Michel (1492). Turn right along the Quais Richelieu/Douane/Louis XVIII for the beautiful tree-lined Esplanade des Quinconces, laid out in the 1820s. (Half-way along the Quai Richelieu glance left for the medieval PORTE CAILHAU.) The ESPLANADE DES QUINCONCES, one of Europe's largest and finest public squares, has good parking. It occupies the site of the medieval fortress built by Charles VII of France to intimidate the citizenry after 'liberating' them from English rule in 1453.

The Celtic settlement known to the Romans as Burdigala became the capital of the Roman province of Aquitania. The renowned Latin poet, statesman and wine-lover Ausonius was a native. In the fourth century an archbishopric was established here. In the eleventh it became a major city of the dukes of Aquitaine but the marriage of Eleanor of Aquitaine to Henry Plantagenet, King of England from 1154, began a 300-year association with England, during which the region of the Bordelais and Gascony became one of the greatest wine-producing regions of France, thanks to the English trade. In the 1350s and '60s Bordeaux was capital of a province governed by Edward the Black Prince (d. 1368), whose son, Richard 'of Bordeaux' (born here), became Richard II of England. The Porte Cailhau, near the Place du Palais, is all that remains of the Château de l'Ombrière, centre of the English administration. The university was founded in 1441 but, after demonstrations in favour of the English connection, in 1453 the English were finally expelled. In the sixteenth century there were street demonstrations demanding a return to the 'good old days' of the English regime. In the 1600s Bordeaux tended to oppose Paris but in the following century the flourishing city was transformed by some of Europe's most elegant urban planning, inspired chiefly by officials appointed from Paris. During the Revolution Bordeaux supported the moderates; its deputies in the National Assembly headed the group known as the 'Girondistes' (from the Gironde). In the later nineteenth century the region became favoured by English expatriates and it was here that Rugby Union entered France. In 1871 a new national assembly established the Third Republic at its session in the Bordeaux's Grand Théâtre. During June 1940 Bordeaux was the seat of the French government following France's capitulation to Germany. Bordeaux has an International Trade Fair and a major music festival, the *Mai Musical*.

Leaving the Esplanade des Quinconces by the Cours du 30 Juillet, you come to the Place de la Comédie, Bordeaux's central square, dominated by the 1770s GRAND THÉÂTRE with its colonnaded façade and classical statues of muses and goddesses. The great staircase has a cupola over the well and the historic circular auditorium should be seen. Admire the lovely vista down the Allées de Tourny (off to the right), then, crossing the Cours Chapeau Rouge, follow the smart shopping street R. Ste Catherine to the old town (pedestrian precincts). At the Cours d'Alsace et Lorraine, cross over for the R. des Ayres. Turn left past St. Paul's Church (1676) and then right down the narrow R. St James for the GROSSE CLOCHE, the most dramatic relic of the English period. Built in the fifteenth century, the lofty double-towered gateway with its great clock today retains a special place in the affections of the city, being the place where the start of the grape harvest is proclaimed. Turn right along the Cours

Victor Hugo, past a market, on to the Cours Pasteur and turn right again for the TOUR PEY BERLAND, named after the archbishop who built it in the 1440s, and the CATHÉDRAL ST ANDRÉ.

Behind the thirteenth-century Porte Royale with its fine statuary, you enter the aisleless nave (begun in the twelfth century). The imposing choir, begun in the 1300s by Bertrand de Got, the archbishop of Bordeaux who later became Pope Clément V (*Avignon), shows marked similarities to the English 'Decorated' style. The choir, with its fascinating MISERICORDS, and also the transepts, were completed during the last decades of English rule.

There is a number of important museums near the Cathedral. The R. Vital Carles, running up from the N. side, leads to the MUSEUM OF THE RESISTANCE in the Centre J. Moulin. Opposite the Cathedral's W. front stands the former archbishop's palace (1780s), now the Hôtel de Ville, open afternoons. Beyond this, flanking the pretty Jardins de la Mairie, are the Musée d'Aquitaine (local history) and the MUSÉE DES BEAUX-ARTS. Its extensive collection from most of Europe's major national schools includes fine works by Veronese, Rubens, the pastellist Quentin de la Tour, Reynolds, Delacroix, Matisse, and sculptures by Rodin. A block away, up the R. Bouffard, is the Musée des Arts Decoratifs (furniture, ceramics, arms and armour, and miniatures). Follow the R. Bouffard to the Place Gambetta, a classic example of eighteenth-century Bordeaux (and also the site of the city's guillotine during the Revolutionary Terror). From here the Cours Intendant (Goya died at no. 57) will bring you back to the Place de la Comédie.

CAHORS

Route (Bergerac): D.660 via Monpazier and Villefranche-du-Périgord to the junction with the D.911
Distance: 107 km (67 mi)
Medieval walled town; Valentré bridge; local wine; a magnificent drive through classic Dordogne landscapes.

The capital of Quercy, Cahors is famous for its deeply lustrous full-bodied red wine, known as the 'black' wine of Cahors. There are numerous good restaurants serving traditional local dishes with the truffles and *foie gras* for which the region is renowned. The old quarter, SE of the Place Aristide Briand, has been well restored.

The D.911 brings you in to the Barbacane gate in the medieval RAMPARTS, which defended the neck of the peninsula formed by the River Lot on which the town stands. To your left notice the fifteenth-century Tour St Jean. Follow the road system to the Place de Gaulle. Across the road stands a Roman arch, known as the Porte de Diane, the Tour de Jean XXII (named after the early fourteenth-century pope born here) and, beyond that, the tower of the Church of St Barthélemy. You continue along the Boulevard Gambetta, named after the great republican statesman Léon Gambetta (1838-82), also born in Cahors, and pass the old bishop's palace on your right in the Parc Tassart, now the town museum. A little further on the R. Foch leads (left) to the Cathedral, or you can continue on across the R. du Président Wilson, with the Hôtel de Ville on your left, to the Place A. Briand and the S.I.

Return to the Hôtel de Ville and left along the R. Président Wilson (Gambetta was born at no. 9) for the famous PONT VALENTRÉ. Dating from the first decade of the fourteenth century, it carries the road over the River Lot on six arches rising from sturdy piers, tapering like boat prows upstream to break the current. Although somewhat over-restored in the late nineteenth century it remains one of the finest medieval bridges in Europe and is certainly very dramatic. The approach is guarded by battlemented gateways and the bridge itself is fortified with three slim towers, capped with pyramid-shaped tiled roofs, two equipped with machicolations. It has, not surprisingly, featured more than once on the wine labels of the district. Cross the river for a fine view of bridge and town.

Approaching the twelfth-century CATHÉDRAL DE ST ÉTIENNE one is immediately impressed by the two huge masonry drums which support the cupolas over the nave. The W. front has some good sculpture, but the Ascension scene over the North Portal, which is flanked by the Apostles, is done with a true sense of drama. Inside there are some good fourteenth-century paintings in the first cupola and in the choir. The cathedral complex also includes the late medieval cloister, chapter house and archdeaconry. There are some fine old houses on the riverside quay behind the Cathedral; on the other bank, across the nineteenth-century Pont Neuf, stands the fifteenth-century Church of the Sacred Heart. Follow the Quai Champollion down to the medieval church of St Urcisse and the narrow streets of the OLD QUARTER. (R. Blanqui and R. D.E. Brives both lead back to the Boulevard Gambetta.)

ST ÉMILION

Route (Bergerac): D.936 then D.122
Distance: 56 km (35 mi)

Surrounded by one of the world's most famous wine districts, St Émilion is an enchanting old town with precipitous streets, stepped alleyways and ancient archways.

Approaching along the D.122 you come to car parks outside ruined stretches of the old town walls (some 300 m/300 yds away to your right stands the fourteenth-century BRUNET GATE). However it is probably better to turn left along the R. de la Madeleine and then hairpin right for the Promenade, with the ramparts on your right and the Château du Roi behind them.

The fourth-century Latin poet Ausonius, a native of *Bordeaux, had a vineyard here, possibly on the domain of the modern Château Ausone, the leading Premier Grand Cru Classé of the district. However, the town's name derives not from its Roman connections but from a Breton hermit, Émilion, who made his retreat here in the eighth century. In the later Middle Ages 'Semilione' was under English rule and one of the loyalist towns of English Gascony. In 1199 it received its charter from King John, which allowed it to elect its own magistrates or '*Jurats*'. A series of royal enactments from Edward I (1289) to Edward III (1341) defined the boundaries of the district and it was ordained that every wine offered for sale as 'St Émilion' had to be passed by the Jurats and branded with the town arms. The modern *appellation contrôlée* territory has virtually the same boundaries as those laid down by the English kings. Every autumn the Jurats assemble on the TOUR DU ROI, the lofty keep of the castle built under Henry III of England in the 1220s, to declare the opening of the grape harvest. Every spring, dressed in their fur-trimmed robes of office, they go in solemn procession to the Monolithic Church to determine that the previous year's vintage is worthy of their seal of approval.

You may start your tour at the ÉGLISE COLLÉGIALE off the Ave de Verdun. The fine fourteenth-century N. portal with its Last Judgement is sadly mutilated. Within, the twelfth-century Romanesque nave leads to a lofty Gothic thirteenth-century choir; notice the twelfth-century murals of the Virgin and St Catherine. The adjacent cloister can be seen on application to the S.I. in the Place des Créneaux. It has an interesting collection of old wine-making instruments.

Now descend to the marketplace and the café tables in the square for the remarkable subterranean ÉGLISE MONO-LITHIQUE (monolithic church). Excavated from the grottoes and caves in the rock from the ninth to the twelfth centuries, it would make an excellent wine cellar were it not a church. The fourteenth-century portal is handsomely carved with a Last Judgement and a scene of the Resurrection of the Dead. The rugged, rock-hewn pillars and vaulting of the interior create a dramatic effect. Nearby is the early thirteenth-century Trinity Church and below that the grotto traditionally considered the Hermitage Cell of St Émilion and the catacombs hewn in the rock. Now take the R. Cadène to the picturesque old PORTE CADÈNE (literally a chained gate, from the chains put across it at night).

Trips from the
CAMARGUE

ARLES

Aigues Mortes	50 km (31 mi)
Aix-en-Provence	75 km (47 mi)
Avignon	37 km (22 mi)
Lyon	TGV
Marseille	93 km (58 mi)
Nîmes-Pont du Gard–Châteauneuf-du-Pape–Orange	round trip approx. 160 km (100 mi)

Roman amphitheatre; Roman theatre; Cathedral of St Trophime and cloister; Roman cemetery; Alyscamps; Roman baths.

Start at LES ARÈNES, the Roman amphitheatre, which is a 1-km (½-mi) walk from the railway station or rather less from the car park in the Place Lamartine (where in 1888-9 Van Gogh shared a house with Gauguin). The largest Roman amphitheatre north of the Alps, Les Arènes comprises two tiers of 60 arches with an outer circuit of some 460 m (1510 ft). For much of the Middle Ages it *was* the town of Arles, with some 200 houses and public buildings clustering up the terracing within the protective ring of massive masonry. Three towered defensive gateways guarded access. As late as the 1700s the arena was still congested with 'beggarly tenements'. Today, seating more than 20,000 spectators, it is used for bullfights.

Founded by the Greek city of Masalia (*Marseille) in the sixth century BC, Arles overtook its mother city as a port during the fourth decade BC, thanks to its support for Julius Caesar, the victor in Rome's civil war, and to a canal dug to the Golfe de Fos. Converted to Christianity in the first century AD, supposedly by St Trophimus, a disciple of Paul, it hosted major church councils once Christianity was adopted as the religion of the empire by Constantine the Great (d. 337), whose son, Emperor Constantine II, was born

here. Taken by Germanic invaders in the fifth century, it fell
in the mid-700s to Saracen sea rovers, who established
numerous bases in the Provençal hinterland. Seat of an
archbishopric it was even, from 879, capital of a kingdom
known variously as the kingdom of Burgundy, of Provence
and of Arles. In the eleventh century the kingdom was
incorporated into the Holy Roman Empire, though control
was ceded to the French kings in the fourteenth century. Arles
retained a special status within France until the French
Revolution abolished the archbishopric.

E. of the Arènes stand the Church of Nôtre Dame-de-la-Major and a stretch of the later medieval ramparts. To the SW is the THÉÂTRE ANTIQUE, the Roman theatre, seating 7000 spectators, which is still used for festival productions. Much of the stone seating has been restored, but two Corinthian columns form the original acting area or *skena* (*Orange). Take the R. de la Calade round to the Place de la République, with its ornamental water basin, for the W. front of the Church (formerly cathedral) of ST TROPHIME. The unassuming if lofty façade is abutted on either side by terraced houses. A shallow flight of steps leads up to the projecting portal, gable-roofed with two projecting wings supporting three deeply recessed arches. A superb example of Provençal Romanesque architecture and sculpture, it is richly adorned with figures. The Last Judgement in the tympanum depicts Christ in Glory with the emblems of the Four Evangelists, the saved souls on Christ's right, the damned on his left. Below can be seen the Adoration of the Magi and of the Shepherds and the Massacre of the Innocents. Inside, notice the altar in the N. Transept, a fourth-century sarcophagus with a relief of the Crossing of the Red Sea. A lane near the church leads down to the beautiful ST TROPHIME CLOISTER (twelfth-fourteenth centuries) with many more fine Provençal-style sculptures. Across the Place de la République is the Musée Lapidaire Païen, rich in classical Greek and Roman sculpture and sarcophagi. You may decide to pass on this one but do not miss the ALYSCAMPS (Champs Élysées), a remarkable avenue of antique tombs that once formed the approach to the town. Cross the R. de la République to the Boulevard des Lices (opposite the S.I.) and turn left. The ancient necropolis of Roman Arles, it became one of Europe's most fashionable cemeteries with the burial of St Trophime (Trophimus) here. Mentioned by Dante in the *Inferno*, it once covered several acres.

Returning via the Boulevard des Lices, take the R. Président Wilson for the MUSÉON ARLATE, a fascinating if congested museum of local life and culture. Founded by the Nobel Prize-winning poet Mistral (1830-1914, the pioneer of the revival of Provençal literature), it is packed with photographs, folk musical instruments, costumes and every possible memento of the Arles and Camargue region. Nearby, in the R. Balze, stands the Musée Lapidaire Chrétien, containing Christian sarcophagi and sculptures dating back to the fourth century. A staircase leads down to the CRYPTO-PORTICUS (first century BC), a labyrinth of galleries built as grain stores and probably the undercroft of the Roman forum. Past the ruins of the palace of the kings of Provence and the Hôtel de Ville, the modern Place du Forum offers inviting cafés and a statue of Mistral. Continuing on towards the river you will come to the impressive ruins of the ROMAN BATHS and, beyond, the Musée Réattu named after a local artist (d. 1833). Besides paintings of local interest, this contains drawings by Picasso and twentieth-century tapestries by Jean Lurçat (*Angers).

AIGUES MORTES

Route (Arles): D.570 – Les Bruns, continue for about 5 km (3 mi), then D.58
Distance: 50 km (31 mi)
(About 10 km (6 mi) out of Arles you will pass the Mas du Pont due Rousty, which houses the Camargue Museum)
Landscape; medieval ramparts; seaside resorts of Le Grau du Roi and Port Camargue.

After leaving the D.570 you cross the Petit Rhône river into the Plain of Aigues Mortes, with its salt marshes and wild horses. After crossing the Canal du Rhône à Sète, you make a sharp left turn at the 1240s Tour Carbonière, built as an advance defence to the town, some 3 km (2 mi) ahead. The name, Aigues Mortes, means dead (or stagnant) waters, but the town, lying almost mirage-like across the marshy plains, was once a bustling port. Its ramparts, almost intact after 700 years, offer an evocative glimpse of Europe at the time of the crusaders.

A medieval new town, Aigues Mortes was founded by King St Louis IX to provide an embarkation port for his planned crusade. The royal writ did not run in this part of southern France and the site, a fishing village on a marshy sea coast, was given by a local monastery. Defensive works were essential. The circular Constance Tower, with its pinnacled watch tower overlooking the NW walls, was the first building. From the ground-floor guardroom with the garrison bread oven, you climb to the Hall of the Knights, past a minute oratory chapel built in the thickness of the wall. Climb the turret for a splendid panorama of the town and the immense plain, bounded to the NW by the foothills of the Cévennes.

As you walk the ramparts (about half an hour) note the grid-iron street plan. Characteristic of many medieval new towns it is, perhaps unexpectedly, almost all that remains of Louis's foundation; the buildings, though old, date from later periods. The King granted wide privileges to attract settlers (as the modern Soviet government does to persuade people to move to new cities in the remoter parts of Siberia). His first crusade sailed in 1248 for Egypt; it failed and the King was captured. Ransomed home, he made a second expedition and then, in 1270, a third, again from Aigues Mortes, dying of the plague in Tunis. Building continued (the ramparts were completed about 1300) and the place became an administrative centre as royal power grew in the region. The new port also needed protection from the sea rovers of the Mediterranean; the southern wall fronted a sea-water basin and is pierced by five gates and posterns which gave on to the quays. From here a canal was dug to give a secure deep-water channel to the sea at Le Grau du Roi. Over the centuries the sea has retreated some 8 km (5 mi) from the old crusader port. It declined and has only revived in this century. But the echoes of its heroic past still linger.

Round off these few hours down by the sea, or return to the Tour Carbonière for the D.62 to Montpellier (40 km, 25 mi), with its great art gallery, the Musée Fabre and majestic Promenade du Peyrou parade.

AIX-EN-PROVENCE

**Route (Arles): N.453/N.113 to Salon-de-Provence, then A.7/
       A.8**
Distance: 75 km (47 mi)
**Cours Mirabeau, 'one of Europe's most beautiful streets';
cathedral; tapestry museum; Cézanne's studio; music festival
(July and August).*

From Arles leave the A.8 at the junction with the N.8, to
enter the town along the Ave des Belges for the Place du
Général de Gaulle (from the rail station take the Ave Victor
Hugo for the Place). The S.I. is on the Place and the old
casino lies a short walk up the Boulevard de la République.
    Aix is a town for the idler. From the Place de Gaulle, with
its nineteenth-century fountain, the restaurants and pavement cafés of the COURS MIRABEAU invite immediate
patronage. Two double rows of great plane trees roof the
street and its handsome seventeenth- and eighteenth-century

buildings with a dappling canopy against the lazy southern sun. Half-way up is the Fontaine Chaude (on which a natural hot spring bubbles over carved, moss-covered rocks) and at the top stands a fountain by the nineteenth-century sculptor David d'Angers with a statue of the medieval ruler of Provence, 'Good King René', holding a bunch of grapes in his hand.

The hot mineral springs here were famous in Celtic times. In 122 BC the Roman general Sextius founded Aquae Sextiae ('the Waters of Sextius'). The town became the seat of an archbishopric in the fifth century; and of the court of the counts of Provence in the twelfth. Patrons of the troubadours, they presided over a brilliant and independent culture, which was crushed in the early 1200s during the Albigensian 'Crusade' led by northern French barons. The fifteenth century was another golden age. The university was founded (1409) and from 1443 the 1440s Aix was the capital of the polymath, dilettante and devotee of chivalry, René, duke of Anjou, count of Provence and titular king of Jerusalem and Naples, always known as Good King René (1409-80). No politician, René was forced to nominate the French king Louis XI his heir in Anjou and when his son died in 1486 Provence, also, was annexed by France. Aix came to national prominence during the French Revolution when in 1789 it elected the impressive ugly and notoriously extravagant Honoré, comte de Mirabeau (1749-91), as its representative to the Third Estate. The celebrated populist orator was later to be suspected of dealings with the court and would no doubt have ended his life on the guillotine had he not died first of his excesses.

From the Cours Mirabeau the R. du 4e Septembre leads to the Musée Paul Arbaud (local art and history) and the richly carved sixteenth-century Hôtel de Boisgelin in the square of the beautiful 'Four Dolphins Fountain' (1667). Take the R. Cardinale for the MUSÉE GRANET, named after the local painter François Granet, with paintings by him, many fine old masters (including a Rembrandt self-portrait) and a Cézanne gallery. Nearby is the thirteenth-century Church of St John of Malta (within, a reconstruction of the tomb of the Counts of Provence, destroyed in the Revolution). Turn left along the R. d'Italie and right at R. de l'Opéra for some fine houses and, at no. 28, the BIRTHPLACE OF CÉZANNE.

Return to the Cours Mirabeau and the 'Moss' fountain for the R. Clemenceau. At Place St Honoré turn left for the cobbled Place d'Albertas and its fountain; then the R. d'Aude and R. Maréchal to the seventeenth-century fine baroque Hôtel de Ville. The town hall square is the scene of a weekly flower market grouped round the fountain and the sixteenth-century wrought-ironwork clock tower. The continuations of the R. du Maréchal Foch bring you to the excellent folklore collections of the MUSÉE DU VIEIL AIX ('Old Aix') and the CATHEDRAL OF ST SAUVEUR, a fascinating if unclassifiable compound of architectural styles. Inside are a number of fine paintings, notably the mysterious, symbolic 'Burning Bush' of Nicholas Froment. It depicts the Virgin and Child seated in the bosky canopy of a great 'bush' of trees set on a mountain rock with a remote landscape far below – Good King René's portrait is in the left panel of the triptych, his wife Jeanne's in the right. Adjacent to the Cathedral stands the largely seventeenth-century palace of the archbishops, now the TAPESTRY MUSEUM and in July and August the venue for performances of the music festival. Do not miss the delightful little cathedral cloister. For CÉZANNE'S STUDIO continue over the Boulevard Aristide Briand along the Ave Pasteur for the Ave Paul Cézanne.

[Before leaving the cathedral area you can follow the R. du Bon Pasteur, skirting the university building to reach the Spa building with its Roman bath, and beyond that along the R. Célony to the beautiful gardens of the Pavilion Vendôme.]

Devotees of Cézanne's paintings should try to find time for the 16-km (10-mi) drive out along the Vauvenargues road to the Montaigne St Victoire; enthusiasts of modern art should not miss the Vasarely Foundation some 3½ km (2½ mi) out along the Ave des Belges.

AVIGNON

Route (Arles): N.570
Distance: 37 km (22 mi)
Medieval ramparts; Palace of the Popes; the Bridge of St Bénézet, the Pont d'Avignon of the nursery rhyme.

Approaching from Arles along the 570 you pass under the railway just before the Porte St Michel. Swing left along the Boulevard Saint Roch outside the ramparts, follow the ring road round to the Porte de l'Oulle and then follow the signs up to the central subterranean car park with its pedestrian exits on the Place du Palais. If you arrive by train, walk through the ramparts into the Cours Jean Jaurès. Passing the S.I. (R. Fabre), continue to the shady Place de l'Horloge with its fourteenth-century clock tower incorporated into the nineteenth-century town hall. The site of the town's Roman forum, it is still a hub of local life with busy pavement cafés and restaurants – the Auberge de France (1 Michelin star) is noted for its regional dishes.

Set in a landscape of olive groves, Avignon dates back to Gallo-Roman times. In the Middle Ages it was virtually an independent republic bordering the papal territory of Comtat Venaissin. In 1309, looking for a haven from the turbulent politics of Rome, the French pope Clement V moved the papal see to Avignon. For almost 70 years – the second 'Babylonish captivity' – a succession of French popes ruled here. Petrarch, who lived in Avignon from 1313 to 1337, condemned the corruption of the town of the popes as a sink of vice. Pope Gregory moved back to Rome but when he died the following year (1378) the French cardinals, refusing to accept his Italian successor, elected a rival pope who moved back to Avignon. The 'Great Schism' which followed divided Europe between two (at times even three) popes for the next 40 years. Avignon remained a papal dependency until the French Revolution.

The massive PALAIS DES PAPES, sacked by the revolutionaries, was used as a prison and later an army barracks, until restoration work began in the early 1900s. It was built in two stages: the fortress-like Old Palace to the north between 1335 and 1342 and the New Palace, completed in 1352. Entering by the Champeaux Gate you come to the

Grand Courtyard; a ramp on your left takes you round to the Benedict XII cloister, overlooked by the papal apartments and by the Consistory Hall (on the E. side). On the first floor is the Banqueting Hall, adorned with eighteenth-century Gobelins tapestries (it had been the home of papal legates from the sixteenth century to 1791). St Martial's Chapel, with fine mid-fourteenth-century Italian frescoes, gives off the Hall. Through the Robing Room you come to the papal bedchamber, delightfully painted with birds and vines. The adjacent 'Stag Chamber' (*Chambre du Cerf*) has a handsome wood ceiling and wall paintings of hunting scenes. From there you continue into the immense Clementine Chapel and then go down to the Great Audience and Lesser Audience Chamber on the ground floor. You leave the Palace via the guardroom and the Champeaux gate.

The Cathedral of Nôtre Dame des Doms (twelfth-century but heavily restored and altered) stands next to the Palace. The magnificent fourteenth-century tomb of Pope John XXII may well be the work of an English master known to have been working here at the time. The Cathedral also contains a fine twelfth-century marble episcopal throne. The Rocher des Doms park adjacent to the cathedral gives a beautiful panorama with the famous bridge below in the foreground, the little town of Villeneuve lès Avignon across the river and away to the NE Mount Ventoux (climbed by the poet Petrarch – perhaps the first recorded instance of mountaineering). Now visit the Petit Palais, the medieval palace of the archbishops of Avignon, with a fifteenth-century façade. It now houses a magnificent collection of paintings (including a Virgin and Child by Botticelli and an altarpiece by Enguerrand Quarton).

The Bridge of St Bénézet, the famous Pont d'Avignon, takes its name from a shepherd who, inspired apparently by divine command, initiated the building in 1177. Volunteers flocked to the site and the work was completed in eight years. One of the piers rested on an island where, it is suggested, the dancing took place – i.e. 'under' (*sous*), not 'on' (*sur*), the bridge. Only four of the spans survive. The little chapel of St Nicholas reflects a common practice in the Middle Ages when bridge-building was considered a work of charity to travellers and hence of piety. The tower on the other bank, in Villeneuve lès Avignon, is the fourteenth-century Tour Philippe le Bel, which once guarded the head of the old bridge. To reach it today you must take the Pont Edouard Daladier. Villeneuve is well worth a visit (see below) and drivers are recommended to use the car to complete their exploration of Avignon. The R. St Agricol, leading out of the Place de l'Horloge, passes the church of the same name with a fine fifteenth-century W. front; turn left on the R. Joseph Vernet for the strangely atmospheric Musée Calvet – some superb paintings from sixteenth-century Breughel to twentieth-century Utrillo, archaeological exhibits and a collection of wrought-iron work. Crossing the R. de la République by the S.I., continue along R. Fabre and R. des Lices for the CLOTH-DYERS' QUARTER, the principal street of which, the cobbled R. des Teinturiers with its old houses, skirts the little River Sorgue where the waterwheels once drove the fullers' mills. (An alleyway leads to the '*Penitents Gris*', a church with a dramatic golden 'glory' from seventeenth-century Peru.) From here the R. de la Masse and the R. du Roi René lead back, past the Church of St Didier with its famous statue of the Virgin and the fourteenth-century Livrée Ceccano tower, to R. de la République. Thence, via the fashionable shopping street Cours Jean Jaurès, you can regain the railway station or the ring road (turn right) for the Pont Edouard Daladier and VILLENEUVE LÈS AVIGNON. This pleasant suburb also has some fine monuments. The view from the Tour Philippe le Bel is dramatic. From here the R. Montée de la Tour leads to the Musée Municipale (a seventeenth-century hospice) with the little-known *Coronation of the Virgin* by the fifteenth-century Avignon master Enguerrand Quarton, one of Europe's most stunning paintings. Also well worth visiting is the CHARTREUSE DU VAL DE BÉNÉDICTION, the venue for exhibitions and other cultural events during July and August; a short walk away is the Fort St André.

LYON

Route (rail): trains leave Arles about 8 a.m. and 10 a.m., journey time about 2¾ hours
Food; old quarter of town; museums.

The Lyonnais boast that their city is the gastronomic capital of France (and by implication the world). It is also said to be at the confluence of three rivers, the Rhône, the Saone and the Beaujolais. Thanks to the excellence of French national railways it is a day-trip from either Paris or Arles. For me, it makes more sense to do the trip from the south. The contrast in style is more marked. If you want a break from the sea, the sunbathing and enervating atmosphere of the Midi, this business-like metropolis, with the superbly polished *haute cuisine* of its great restaurants and their classic burgundies, broadens the horizon of your holiday marvellously. Be prepared for a long (and expensive) day. Only enthusiasts should make this trip: they will have plenty to tell the stay-at-homes that will make even those Camargue horses seem somewhat postcard. Do make an early start. The first morning train from Arles arrives about 10.30, giving you time for some sightseeing before lunch. Afterwards you should have a couple of hours before the evening train home for more tourism – or not, as the case may be.

There are two railway stations at Lyon, the Perrache and the Part Dieu. Not all trains stop at both (check before leaving Arles). The Perrache (the first one) gives on to the Place Carnot, a handsome town concourse with an S.I.

From here it is a ten-minute walk up the R. Victor Hugo to the great central square of Lyon, Place Bellecour. R. du Colonel Chambonnet leads to the Pont Bonaparte and so to the old town, where I recommend you start your visit. The PART DIEU station, despite what others may tell you, is to my mind the more interesting station. Formerly the district was dominated by an army barracks. This has been cleared away and in its place a typically French exercise in city development has been carried out. Fed by the public investment represented by the TGV, a dramatic, if at times overpowering, display of 1970s and 1980s architecture is embodied in public and commercial buildings. They remind the tourist that for France '*le hi-tech*' is as much a part of '*La*

Gloire' as culture and art. There is a tourist information desk on the station concourse where you should get a plan of the old quarter (*le Vieux Lyon*) and of the '*Traboulle*' district (see below). There is a regular bus service from Part Dieu to R. St Jean in the old quarter, where you will find the remains of Roman Lyon, the Cathedral and delightful walks through the old streets.

One of the major cities of Roman Gaul, 'Ludgunum' had a Christian community from the second century, the first in Gaul. Late in the fifth century it became the chief city of the Burgundians, a Germanic tribe which extended its power over much of old Provence. However, it was the archbishops who came to control the city's affairs. In 1274 a great ecumenical Council held in the unfinished cathedral asserted the unity of the Eastern Orthodox and Catholic churches. It did not last! A century or so later saw the establishment of the silk industry and the start of the city's long textile tradition. By the early 1500s it had become noted for fine book printing. Lyon suffered terribly during the Revolution, thousands were 'executed' and much of the city destroyed. Revival came in the early 1800s when the Lyon-born Joseph Jacquard (1752-1834) introduced his power loom (important also for its use of punched cards to control pattern design). Here too was born the great mathematician and pioneer of electricity A.-M. Ampère (1775-1836), and in the 1890s the Lumière brothers of Lyon, pioneers of cinematography, opened a studio in the city. During World War II Lyon was a centre of the Resistance and of the notorious Gestapo HQ under Klaus Barbie, the Butcher of Lyon. Today the city is one of France's leading commercial and industrial centres.

The CATHEDRAL of St Jean ranges in style from late Romanesque to Flamboyant Gothic. Note the thirteenth-century glass in the choir and the transept rose windows; the fourteenth-century astronomical clock (N. transept); the late fifteenth-century carvings in the Bourbon chapel; and the Cathedral treasury. Nearby is the funicular railway station to the ROMAN THEATRES and the remarkable modern structure, much of it underground, housing the Roman museum. (There is also a funicular line up to the grotesque nineteenth-century basilica of Nôtre Dame de Fouvière, certainly a curiosity but worth a visit only, perhaps, for the panoramic view it commands.)

To explore VIEUX LYON follow the R. St Jean from the Cathedral. Alleys and '*traboulles*', vaulted passages, give on to little courtyards, stepped streets and occasional old mansions. The MUSÉE DU VIEUX LYON (turn left at far end of R. St Jean), housed in a magnificent, restored sixteenth-century mansion, is well worth a visit. In the R. du Boeuf, opposite, the Tour Rose RESTAURANT recently won a Michelin star for its *nouvelle cuisine*. A little further up is the Boeuf d'Argent and other recommended restaurants in the old town include Le Comptoir du Boeuf (Place Neuve St Jean) and Les Ardechois (Rue St Jean), both near the Cathedral and reasonably priced.

After your visit to Vieux Lyon you can continue up the bank of the Saone to cross by the Pont de la Feuille to the R. de Constantine and the MUSÉE DES BEAUX-ARTS, on the Place Terreaux near the much restored (seventeenth-century) Hôtel de Ville. The museum's treasure includes works by Gerhardt David, Cranach the Elder, Honthorst, Zurbaran, Philippe de Champagne and Rubens, as well as the French nineteenth- and twentieth-century masters, among them the Lyon-born Puvis de Chavannes. To the north lies the TRA-BOULLE district. As the name suggests, like the old town it is a warren of little streets and passages, a haven of the Resistance during the War. A street plan of the district should be used. RESTAURANTS here include La Mère Brazier (R. Royale), praised a generation ago by Elizabeth David and more recently recipient of a Michelin star. It is expensive. Also recommended is the Pied de Cochon (R. St Polycarpe) and the Léon de Lyon (R. Pléney, near the Museum), 2 Michelin stars.

Three other museums in Lyon cater for specialist interests: the Musée des Arts Decoratifs (R. de la Charité), with not only a fine selection of furniture, tapestries and Lyon ceramic wares from the sixteenth to eighteenth centuries, but also a rare collection of old wallpapers; the Musée Historique des Tissus (textile museum) next door, probably the world's largest collection of tapestries, carpets and fabrics of all kinds from ancient times to the 1900s; and the Musée de l'Imprimerie et de la Banque (printing and banking), in the R. de la Poulaillerie, a little way down from the Beaux-Arts.

MARSEILLE

Route (Arles): N.113 for Salon de Provence, then A.7
Distance: 93 km (58 mi)
Old port; Isle of Château d'If; la Canebière.

From the waterfront of the Old Port, where you can buy
fresh-caught fish from traditional fishing smacks in the centre
of a modern city, to the dramatic hill-top church of Nôtre
Dame de la Garde (view) this great commercial port sustains
a mood of expansive vitality. A boat-trip to the Isle of
Château d'If makes a pleasant diversion.

The A.7 brings you to the Gare St Charles (pay parking).
The station has a pleasant airy concourse with attractive
café-bars. The Boulevard d'Athènes leads to the famous La
Canebière, lined with cafés, restaurants and shops. Formerly
a rope walk (*canabé* = hemp), it takes you past the old
Bourse building, housing the Maritime Museum (intriguing
collection of ship models), and the S.I. to the Quai des Belges
of the OLD PORT.

Founded in about 600 BC by Greek merchant venturers,
'Massalia' established trading outposts at *Arles, *Nice and
Antibes. Under the Romans it suffered for its opposition to
Caesar during the Civil War. Greek and Roman ruins and
remains can be seen behind the Centre Bourse shopping
centre in the Jardin des Vestiges (archaeological garden) and
the nearby Musée Historique de Marseille (including the hull
timbers of a Roman merchant ship). In the 1090s Marseille
provided transports for the Crusades and prospered from
trade with the Holy Land, having its own commercial quarter
in Christian Jerusalem – later, the Knights of Malta built the
St John's Fort N. of the harbour entrance – St Nicholas's Fort
opposite it was designed by Vauban in the 1660s. The
Oriental trade and African slave trade in the eighteenth
century and imperial expansion in North Africa in the
nineteenth swelled the city's prosperity and the first extension
to the port, the Grande Joliette, dates from the 1850s. The
opening of the Suez Canal meant further expansion and
berths for ocean-going liners. During World War II the
Resistance was very active here and large areas of the old
waterfront were demolished in German reprisals, much else
being razed before the occupying garrison capitulated. In the

1960s the city was notorious as a centre for drug-trafficking. Now the Port of Marseille is a blanket term for installations which run for miles to Martigues on the Berre Lagoon and beyond. The French national anthem derives its name of *La Marseillaise* from the fact that it was the marching song of Revolutionary soldiers who marched to Paris in support of the Convention in 1792. Later the city opposed the Parisian Terror, became a centre of royalist sentiments under Napoleon and was one of Bonapartist sentiments under the restored monarchy.

From the Quai des Belges, skirt the harbour by the Quai du Port past the seventeenth-century façade of the Hôtel de Ville. Behind it lies the Musée du Vieux Marseille, with its sixteenth-century faceted stone façade (a large exhibit devoted to Marseille's playing-card factories), and the remains of the Roman docks. Beyond is a warren of streets, the Panier quarter, all that remains of the old Marseille familiar to movie buffs from Pagnol's 1930s 'Marius' trilogy, though much smartened up.

[The R. Caisserie leads back to the quay near the St John Fort and the Gare Maritime docks of the Grande Joliette. Near the nineteenth-century 'Byzantine' Cathédral de la Major stands its eleventh-century Romanesque predecessor. A short but stiff climb brings you to the seventeenth-century Hospice de la Vieille Charité, handsomely restored almshouses used for temporary art exhibitions. You can reach it more or less directly from the Museum of Old Marseille along the Place des Moulins if you want to miss the port and cathedrals.]

In the Panier you will pass some of Marseille's ethnic restaurants, notably North African and Vietnamese. Traditionally, the city is above all associated with the famous (and expensive) southern fish stew, *bouillabaisse* (not, according to the cognoscenti, what it was in the good old days). The Miramar on the Quai du Port is noted for its seafood.

The Quai des Belges is departure point for regular cruises to the ÎLE DU CHÂTEAU D'IF. Its medieval fortress-prison, renowned from Dumas' novel *The Count of Monte Cristo*, held condemned Protestants en route for the galleys during the sixteenth and seventeenth centuries and the opponents of Napoleon III in the nineteenth. Some excursions also take in the Frioul Islands; even on a bright, sunny day the sea can be choppy; you can explore the islands (1½-2 hours) or return from Château d'If by the next boat. From the Cours Étienne d'Orves, an attractively modernized warehouse with covered market and restaurants, the no. 60 bus will run you to Nôtre Dame de la Garde. Whatever you may think of the nineteenth-century Byzantine-style church and its extraordinary votive offerings from generations of sailors, the view out to sea and over the city from its terraces deserves only superlatives. From the church you can walk down the Chemin de Rochas Blanc and R. d'Endome to the Basilica of St Victor. An abbey founded here in the fifth century was sacked in the tenth by Saracen sea raiders: rebuilding began in the 1040s. Fortified and re-worked in the twelfth century, the structure with its battlemented towers looks more like a fortress than a church. The large and numinously atmospheric crypt is the ancient fifth-century basilica. Open for only a few hours each weekday (check exact times with the S.I.), it has catacombs, sarcophagi and third-century (?) relics. From here, the Rampe St Maurice leads down towards the beautiful Jardin du Pharos, with marvellous views to the Old Port.

Returning to the Quai des Belges, you can take the Métro to the Musée des Beaux-Arts, with extensive collections including a gallery devoted to Honoré Daumier (1808-79), born in Marseille, or a bus from La Canebière to the high-rise block L'UNITÉ D'HABITATION, on the outskirts of the city. A formative building in the history of high-rise residential accommodation, it was built by Le Corbusier in 1952 and is as controversial now as it was then. The Métro will also take you back to the St Charles station.

Round trip
NÎMES – PONT-DU-GARD – ORANGE
CHÂTEAUNEUF-DU-PAPE

This itinerary of just over 160 km (100 mi) takes in the four finest Roman monuments in Provence and offers a diversion to one of the world's most famous wine-growing districts. It is open to variations. The wine enthusiast could, I suppose, miss the theatre at Orange for a more complete exploration of the *dégustations*. Alternatively one could divide the whole trip into two – Nîmes and Pont-du-Gard, a short Day 1; Châteauneuf-du-Pape and Orange, an elastic Day 2. The rail traveller is more or less obliged to take the two-trip option.

NÎMES

Route (Arles): N.113
Distance: 31 km (19.5 mi)
Amphitheatre (les Arènes); Maison Carrée, Roman temple and museum.

Approaching along the N.113/Ave Carnot, turn left on R. Nôtre Dame for Les Arènes which, if you arrive by train, is only 1 km (½ mi) from the station, along the impressive Ave Feuchères. The ticket also admits you to the other principal Roman sites described below.

The AMPHITHEATRE, among the best-preserved in the Roman world but only of middling size, could seat some 20,000 spectators. Built about AD 50, it is elliptical in shape and 133 m (434 ft) long. The sockets which held the poles to carry sun awnings can be seen; the attic storey provided seating for slaves; and the arcading on the first floor is unusually complete. As at *Arles, in the Middle Ages the great structure was used as a fortified town and squalid tenements still congested the site in the late eighteenth century. Today it is once again in use and has long been one of the venues for the Provençal bullfighting season. Nearby

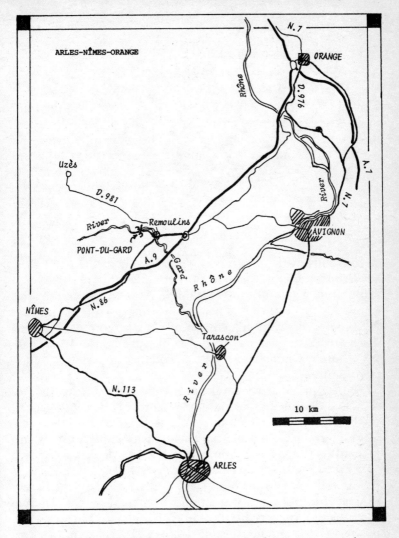

down the R. de la Cité Foulc, the Musée des Beaux-Arts has a huge Roman mosaic on its ground floor.

From the amphitheatre follow the Ave Victor Hugo to the MAISON CARRÉE, built in the first century BC and still in an almost miraculous state of preservation. Since the Renaissance the elegant symmetry of the Greek-style architecture has inspired generations of artists and travellers. Twice as long as it is wide, the building's roof and pediment are supported on 30 Corinthian columns. For two-thirds of it they are engaged

to the walls of the sanctum or '*cella*' while at the front they are free-standing to form the portico. In continuous use since the time it was built, in the Middle Ages the structure was known as the 'capitol' (hence the Provençal name '*capduel*'), the original dedication having been long forgotten. Since the sixteenth century it has served as private house, town hall and church, among other things. Today it houses a museum of antiquities.

The shopping street Boulevard Alphonse Daudet leads to the Quai de la Fontaine and a pleasant walk along the canal to the Jardin de la Fontaine. At the head of the Ave Jean Jaurès, terracing leads up to the water garden of the Spring of Nemausus (the nymph from which the city derives its name) and the ruins of the second-century AD Temple of Diana. From here the Mont Cavalier gardens rise to the Tour Magne, formerly a tower in the Roman defences. Dating from the first century BC, it offers the energetic a magnificent panorama (extending, it is said, to the Pyrenees on a clear day).

An eleventh-century foundation, the Cathedral is unimpressive, and the old quarter of the town equally so. The Musée de Vieux Nîmes (near the Cathedral), however, has some fine furniture and instructive displays devoted to bullfighting in both the Spanish and the Provençal manner. A thriving modern centre of the local wine trade, Nîmes also has an old textile industry – denim, originally 'de Nimes', was invented here.

Before leaving Nîmes you may want to drive or walk up to the fort in the north of the town to see, next to it, the Roman '*castellum*' which was the distribution point for the water brought here by canal from the River Eure, some 40 km (25 mi) away. Now leave town by the R. Nationale/R. Pierre Semard/N.86 for the Pont-du-Gard, the great aqueduct without which the whole system would have been impossible. For the times of the regular coach service enquire at the S.I.

For the PONT-DU-GARD, follow the N.86 for some 20 km (12½ mi), then turn left along the D.981. Built about 19 BC to carry the waters of the River Eure from Uzès to Nîmes, the great aqueduct of honey-coloured stone is among Europe's most majestic and (thanks to nineteenth-century restoration work) most complete Roman monuments – more dramatic in its landscape setting even than that of Segovia. The water channel is carried across the verdant valley of the little River Gardon for a span of 275 m (902 ft), at a height of some 49 m (161 ft) above the river, by three tiers of stone arches. The lowest tier has six arches with piers 6 m (20 ft) thick; the middle tier, 11 arches; the upper tier, carrying the channel, 35 arches. The aqueduct formed one small segment of a roofed stone water channel running for some 40 km (25 m) with an overall gradient of 1:300. It was capable of a daily flow of 20,000 cu m (44 million gallons).

From the car park by the D.981 follow the path under the aqueduct and after about 45 m (50 yds) take the winding path up to the left for a fine view. It is possible to continue up for the walk across the aqueduct, either inside the roofed channel or – at your own risk – along the top. But the scale and beauty of the work are better appreciated from the river valley (the water is startlingly cold). As a precaution against subsidence, the arches were constructed independently. The masonry blocks of the lower course are bound not with mortar but with iron clamps and the span of the arches within each range varies slightly, though perceptibly. The effect, whether thus intended or for engineering considerations, is to imbue the whole ponderous structure with a sense of life.

ORANGE

Route: from Pont du Gard, take the A.9
Roman triumphal arch; Roman theatre.

The motorway exit from the A.9 brings you along R. St
Clément; turn left up Cours A. Briand towards the river,
where you swing right and then left over the bridge for the
Ave de l'Arc, for the triumphal arch.

The Celtic settlement of Arausio was occupied by the
Romans as a colony for veteran soldiers in the third decade
BC. The TRIUMPHAL ARCH, built to commemorate earlier
victories, is outstandingly well preserved. The N. face is
especially notable. Four Corinthian columns flank three
arches; surmounting the pediment of the central arch a relief
frieze depicts the defeat of the Gauls; the scenes are continued
in friezes over the two smaller arches. Other carvings depict
naval victories and files of prisoners. Twelve Corinthian
columns support the entablature, and the arches have coffered ceilings. During the Middle Ages the edifice was
fortified as a defensive tower.

Follow the Ave de l'Arc, over the bridge turn right and then
left down the Cours Aristide Briand to R. St Clément, where
you turn left for the THEATRE. Approaching from this
direction you find, right, the ruins of a Roman gymnasium
and a second-century temple. Claimed to be the best-
preserved Roman theatre in existence, it dates from the last
decade BC and is remarkable for the fact that the lofty stone
skena, the backdrop to the stage itself, is structurally intact,
conveying a sense of what Roman theatricals were like. Three
doorways provide the actors with their exits and their
entrances; the largest is approached by a flight of steps, and
in a niche above it is a statue of the Emperor Augustus, in
whose reign the theatre was built. Apart from two columns
the original facing of the *skena* has disappeared, but Roman
wall paintings allow us to imagine a set adorned with
coloured marble pillars, dramatic masks and statuettes, and a
heavy curtain drape. A vast awning protected the spectators
and the supports from which it was suspended can still be
seen. The back of the *skena* dominates the town's main
square. The semi-circular auditorium, built into the slope of
Mount St Eutropius, could seat some 10,000 spectators.

Parts of the lower five tiers are original. During the Middle Ages the monument was cluttered with houses; today it is once again used as a theatre, for occasional festival productions.

Climb the Montée des Princes d'Orange Nassau for a fine view of the city from the slopes of Mount St Eutropius – the Marcoule atomic energy centre is in the distance.

In the Middle Ages Orange was part of the Holy Roman Empire. By dynastic marriage the principality came to the German family of Nassau with estates also in the Netherlands. The Dutch King of England, William III, was a member of the house of Orange-Nassau, and the present royal family of the Netherlands is descended from it. Orange itself was incorporated into France by the Treaty of Utrecht in 1713.

CHÂTEAUNEUF-DU-PAPE

From the Theatre in Orange follow the N.7/D.950 route signs for 1 km (½ mi) or so and then turn right on the D.68. You should have no difficulty in finding your way to one of the numerous fine *caves* in the region offering *dégustations* of their wine. But do not miss the interesting Père Anselme Museum on the history of wine, where old presses and tools of viticulture are exhibited. The ruins of the popes' castle, from which the place derives its name and which was built by the fourteenth-century popes of Avignon, commands splendid views up the Rhone valley, S. to Avignon and SE to Mont Ventoux.

Leave Châteauneuf-du-Pape by the D.17 for the N.7 to Avignon and thence to Arles.

Trips on the
RIVIERA

Grasse

St Remo

ST RAPHAEL

ST RAPHAEL

Cannes	40 km (25 mi)
Grasse	57 km (36 mi)
Monaco	90 km (56 mi)
Nice	71 km (44 mi)
Aix-en-Provence *Arles*	122 km (74 mi)
St Remo, Italy	134 km (81 mi)

As St Raphael is a terminal of the SNCF Motorail from the Channel ports, and as many heading for the south of France have the beaches here or at St Tropez as their objective, St Raphael is chosen as the point of departure for the day-trips along the Riviera. A favourite resort with the English at the turn of the century, it is protected to the landward side by the Massif de l'Esterel. A pretty, holiday kind of town, its chief attraction is the dramatic CORNICHE DE L'ESTEREL. It has Napoleonic associations, being the place where he landed in 1799 after deserting his army of the Nile and also the port where he embarked for his first exile on the Isle of Elba. A short drive (4 km, 2½ mi) along the N.98 lies FRÉJUS, founded by Julius Caesar and well worth a visit to see the fine Roman amphitheatre.

ST TROPEZ

About 35 km (22 mi) beyond Fréjus, St Tropez is one of the Riviera's most famous and frequented resorts and considered a little too touristy by some. But the beaches are good (and the sea is getting cleaner) and the place certainly throbs with life during the season. Luxury yachts pack the port. From your café table on the Quai G. Péri or Quai Suffren you can see how the other half lives on board. The sixteenth-century CITADEL houses an excellent maritime museum. The ANNONCIADE MUSEUM just beyond the Quai G. Péri has fine work by Matisse, Derain and other twentieth-century artists, while up in the Place Carnot the *boules*-players are in regular session.

The N.7, the principal coast road of the French Riviera, links a string of famous resorts – each of which has its ardent advocates. *Cannes is one of my favourites, with ANTIBES and its picturesque old town only a couple of miles on. Once part of the domains of the Grimaldi rulers of Monaco, it retains memories of the connection in the seaside Château Grimaldi, between the market in Cours Massena and the sea. Today it houses the PICASSO MUSEUM, one of the major collections of the artist's work. The villas of Cap d'Antibes and Juan-les-Pins, still the stamping ground for the mega-rich, recall the Riviera life of the 1920s and 1930s. Next along from Antibes, the lovely resort of CAGNES-SUR-MER boasts a superb RENOIR MUSEUM in the villa of Les Collettes, where the painter spent the last years of his life. Overlooking the town the medieval quarter of Haute-de-Cagnes, with another Grimaldi castle, should not be missed. Next we come to *Nice, *Monaco and finally MENTON. About 105 km (75 mi) from St Raphael and with rather less glitz than the other resorts, it is considered by many the pearl of the Riviera. It too boasts a museum, this time to JEAN COCTEAU, whose decor for the marriage room of the Hôtel de Ville should not be missed. Beyond Menton lies the Italian frontier.

If you want a day-trip 'abroad' from France the frontier town of Ventimiglia, with an extraordinary black-and-chrome-mirrored art deco station bar, is surprisingly worth-while. There are some stunning delicatessens and cheese shops and decent restaurants near the station. The adventurous can aim for SAN REMO, 16 km (12 mi) or so further on into Italy.

The distances in this section are given as from St Raphael. If your holiday base is St Tropez you must add another 35 km (22 mi). If you are staying elsewhere along the Riviera the distances are correspondingly shorter but the route remains the N.7 or, for long-distance journeys, the A.8 autoroute, a few miles inland but roughly parallel to it.

CANNES

Route (St Raphael): N.7 or A.8
Distance: 40 km (25 mi)
Old town 'le Suquet'; Promenade de la Croisette; the port;
Îles des Lerins.

Behind the glitter, the high life and the tourist kitsch, a gentle air of Victorian elegance lingers here and there. The Old Port, brilliant with yachts and luxury cruisers, has elegantly stylish sidewalk cafés, while the beaches are beautiful if congested. Each May the Film Festival swells the little town with the brash bezazz of the international publicity circuit, but Cannes despite this and other media festivals still breathes an endearing and comfortable charm.

Approaching along the N.7 (or the A.8), head for the railway station, where there is car parking and an S.I. From here take the R. Venizélos, R. de la Pompe for the Place Général Charles de Gaulle (pavement café) to the Allées de la Liberté.

The obscure fishing village of Cannes was 'discovered', by chance, in 1814 by the British Lord Chancellor, Lord Brougham, while en route for the winter season at *Nice, then an Italian town. Turned back at the frontier because of a cholera epidemic in Provence, he bought land just W. of Cannes and built a villa. English high society followed, then the speculative builders and then, in the 1860s, the railway. The Anglican Church of Holy Trinity (archdiocese of Gibraltar) in the R. Canada still survives from the high days of 'English' Cannes.

The Allées de la Liberté, gay with its morning FLOWER

MARKET and solemn with the business of the *boules*-players, still commemorates Brougham with a plaque on its fountain. Cross the road to the Pantiéro quay of the OLD PORT. Nearby is the departure point for boat trips to the Îles des Lerins (see below). To your right is the Quai St Pierre with attractive cafés; to your left the Jetée Albert Edouard (i.e. Edward Prince of Wales, later King Edward VII). This runs past the Convention Centre (site of the old Municipal Casino) with an S.I., and ends at a mole protecting the harbour. From here you can gain the beach or cross the Esplanade des Alliés to the palm-lined Promenade de la CROISETTE, with its luxury hotels and bars overlooking the sands and marinas.

The Quai St Pierre leads round to the Boulevard Jean Hibert, overlooking the Plage du Midi beach. Or take the little R. du Port across the R. Clémenceau to climb the oleander-lined streets up to the old town, LE SUQUET. A delightful stroll, it brings you to the modest antiquities of Cannes, the fourteenth-century Tour Suquet, the little Musée la Castre (in the old citadel) and the Church of Nôtre Dame de l'Espérance, with a small Romanesque chapel nearby. From here the R. de la Boucherie leads down to the busy market of Forville. Flowers, fruit and vegetables, fish, shell-fish and cheese are piled on the stalls of the market traders. Alternatively, you can assemble a picnic lunch fit for a gourmet from the delicatessens and charcuteries in the R. Meynadier and the alleys giving off it. A short walk brings you back to the Pantiéro quay for the ferry to the ÎLES DES LERINS.

The Isle of Ste Marguerite (about 15 minutes away) is famous for its seventeenth-century fortress where 'The Man in the Iron Mask' was imprisoned on the orders of Louis XIV from 1687 to 1698 (he died in the Bastille in 1703). The mask was probably made of black silk or velvet but the man's identity is one of history's most fascinating enigmas. The most enticing of the numerous theories is that he was the twin brother of the king himself. The dense oak woods of the island offer delightful walks, and at the W. end of the island are a garden restaurant (walk left from the landing jetty) and remains of a Roman fort. The Isle of St Honorat, less frequently visited, is preferred by some visitors.

GRASSE

Route (St Raphael): N.7 to Cannes, N.85
Distance: 57 km (36 mi)
Dramatic old hill town; perfumeries; Place aux Aires, town square.

As you climb up from the coast the mountain panorama laid out ahead begins to close in, the road snakes round beetling declivities swathed in pines and rocky cliffs steeple to the sky. Approaching the town centre you come to a school at a Y-junction; turn left here, then hairpin right into the Boulevard Victor Hugo and thence to the Boulevard Jeu de Ballon. At the merging of the two roads you glimpse to the right a car park and (below) the JARDIN DES PLANTES public garden. It is best to carry on to the bus station and the parking there. The S.I. is nearby and a street plan is advisable.

In the early Middle Ages Grasse was for a time an independent republic and the seat of a bishopric before being absorbed into the county of Provence in the thirteenth century. An Italian established the perfumery business here in the 1500s and it soon became famous. An eighteenth-century visitor described the gardens, 'whose roses are a great article for the famous *otter* [i.e. 'attar of roses']. They say that 1500 flowers go to a single drop ... in addition there are tuberoses, rosemary, lavender, bergamot and oranges and half Europe is supplied with essences from hence.'

From the car park at the bus station stroll back along the JEU DE BALLON, the town's main street, to the Hôtel de Pontèves, housing the maritime museum devoted mainly to the eighteenth-century Amiral de Grasse, born in the commune. Nearby you come to the PARFUMERIE FRAGONARD, where a guided tour comprises an intriguing display of old copper stills and other apparatus and ingredients of perfume manufacture. The Musée de Fragonard, in a seventeenth-century villa, is attractive but unfortunately the paintings are copies; the panels done for Louis XV's mistress Mme du Barry are now in the Frick Museum, New York. A native of Grasse, Jean-Honoré Fragonard (1732-1806) made his name at Versailles and sought sanctuary from the Revolution here (the house belonging to his cousin, a perfume manufacturer) in 1790. Next to it in the R. Mirabeau the

Musée d'Art et d'Histoire de Provence has excellent collections of furniture as well as objects demonstrating the decorative arts, local folklore and history. Retrace your steps to the beginning of the R. J. Ossola. Passing fine old town houses on your right (Fragonard was born at no. 23), turn right at the R. Tracastel for a steep descent and dramatic views of the town hall and former cathedral (formerly the bishop's palace). Founded about 1200, the Church of Nôtre Dame de Puy has a cumbersome solidity but contains three early paintings by Rubens and *Christ Washing the Feet of His Disciples* by Fragonard, something of a rarity from an artist famed for his *galanteries* and courtly scenes. Behind the church in the Place du 24 Août stands the thirteenth-century Tour de l'Orloge, once the tower of the independent 'consulate' of Grasse, with quite stunning views over the countryside.

We now make our way back up the town heading for the Place aux Aires. R. de l'Evèche, Place de la Poissonerie, R. Mougin Roquefort and a dog-leg at R. M. Journet to R. des Moulinets is one route. But this is where the street plan comes in handy; allow time to explore the steep, narrow alleys and streets – and a little time for recovering your bearings. One of the loveliest little squares in France, the PLACE AUX AIRES feels like the courtyard of a great mansion. Complete with fountain, busy morning flower market and café tables packed under the eighteenth-century arcading, it is the natural place to recover from your exertions in climbing the town. Touristy it undoubtedly is – Moroccan and other pedlars will pester you to buy leather goods and what not – but then if, like me, you are prepared to admit to being a tourist, this is part of the deal. The R. du Thouron will bring you back to the Boulevard Jeu de Ballon; turn right for the car park and bus station.

MONACO

Route (St Raphael): N.7 or A.8
Distance: 90 km (56 mi)
Palace; oceanographic museum; casino.

World-renowned for its casino at Monte Carlo and for the Monaco Grand Prix, when the streets are closed for Europe's most colourful and dramatic Formula 1 motor race, Monaco is technically a sovereign enclave within France. In fact since a treaty of 1918 French approval has been required for the succession to the throne and the cynic can be forgiven for regarding the mini-principality (all of 150 hectares in extent) as little more than a tax haven. Nevertheless, a sovereign state it remains.

There was an ancient Phoenician settlement here known to the Greeks as Monoikos. Genoa built a fort here about AD 1200 and in the fourteenth century the Genoese Grimaldi family made themselves lords of the place. The male line died out in the 1710s but the French nobleman who married the heiress adopted the name. Annexed to France during the Revolution, Monaco was assigned to the Italian kingdom of Sardinia by the Congress of Vienna in 1814 but regained its independence in 1861. Prince Albert I (1889-1922) granted the constitution. In 1949 the 26-year-old Prince Rainier came to the throne and his marriage to the American film star Grace Kelly was the glamour event of 1956. She was tragically killed in a car crash in 1982.

Start your tour at the PALACE, where the changing of the guard takes place just before noon. The original medieval fortress has been transformed over the centuries. There are guided tours from July to September. As well as portraits of the Grimaldi family there is *The Music Lesson*, attributed to Giorgione. A new wing houses a Napoleon Museum. The R. Basse leads to an interesting museum of costume, the Historial des Princes de Monaco, in which waxwork tableaux depict episodes in the family's history. Nearby, in the seventeenth-century Misericord Chapel, you can see the Image of Christ paraded through the streets on Good Friday.

The late-nineteenth-century, Romanesque-style Cathedral houses the Grimaldi tombs, among them that of Princess Grace. There is also a Pietà attributed to Louis Bréa. Down through the delightful St Martin Gardens you come to the renowned OCEANOGRAPHIC MUSEUM founded in 1910 by Prince Albert I (1889-1922), a noted amateur marine biologist. Under the directorship of Jacques Cousteau from 1957, it has displays covering all aspects of oceanography and a superb aquarium.

Now return to the Place d'Armes. The Ave du Port leads down to the waterfront, a gala sight with its luxury cruisers. A bus ride will take you to the Jardin Éxotique, noted for its collection of cacti and splendid PANORAMA of the beautiful bay on which Monaco stands. Here too is the museum of prehistoric anthropology and, below, the stalactite caves of the Grottes de l'Observatoire. Now take a bus to the Place du Casino (S.I.).

The first CASINO was a house on the seafront run by the Société de Bains de Mer, which closed its doors at dusk. Prim rather than profitable, it was moved to its present site in 1862 and the following year the concession passed to a new management. Prospects increased rapidly with the coming of the railway in 1868. A new casino was built (to the designs of Charles Garnier, architect of the Paris Opéra) and a residential development called Monte Carlo ('Mount Charles') after the reigning prince. For 40 years until his death in 1927 Camille Blanc managed the company. In 1954 it was acquired by Aristotle Onassis: today it is nominally under the control of the Monégasque government. To see the luxurious salons and the decor of the bar you need risk no more of your money than the entrance charge.

From the foot of the bluff on which the casino stands, the Ave Princess Grace leads to the villa housing the intriguing Galea Collection of puppets, dolls and automata. From here an elevator will take you up to the Boulevard des Moulins, whence a bus will run you down to the port.

Apart from the casino, Monaco is known for various festivals and for the opera house adjoining the casino, home during the 1920s of Diaghilev's Ballets Russes and during the 1930s of Colonel de Basil's Company.

NICE and CIMIEZ

Route (St Raphael): N.7 or A.8
Distance: 71 km (44 mi)
Old town; Promenade des Anglais; Chagall Museum; Matisse Museum; Roman amphitheatre.

The history of Nice as a resort dates back to at least the mid-1700s. In 1789 the English traveller Arthur Young found a prosperous town with new houses and new streets going up, 'owing very much to the resort of foreigners, principally English, who pass the winter here'. He also found the locals 'dismally alarmed ... that the disturbances at present in France will prevent the English coming this winter.' The 'disturbances' were the French Revolution and Nice was at that time an Italian city. The flavour of Italy still lingers here and there in the old town. The Italian patriot hero Garibaldi (1807-82) was born here, near the old port.

The Italian connection went back to Roman times. In the second century BC the Romans conquered the Greek trading post of Nike ('Victory') and made the old Celtic hill fort of Cemenelum overlooking the harbour the site of their new town. Roman remains are still to be seen at modern Cimiez, where it is recommended you start your visit.

The approach is along the coast road through Nice proper. Coming in from the W. on the N.7 you enter the town along the Promenade des Anglais. You will pass the Ave des Baumettes leading to the Musée des Beaux-Arts Jules Cheret, a collection of predominantly nineteenth-century French art and above all paintings by Cheret (1836-1942), a pioneer of the poster as an art form. Next you pass the grounds of the Musée Massena, with memorabilia of Garibaldi, costumes and displays from Nice carnivals, and paintings. The Promenade ends at the Jardin Albert 1er (S.I.). If you wish to enjoy the morning FLOWER MARKET in the Cours Saleya continue along the promenade (now the Quai des États-Unis) to the grandiloquent nineteenth-century Opera House, where you turn left. The best route to Cimiez lies along the Ave de Verdun to the Place Massena (bus station nearby) where you turn left up the Ave J. Médecin towards the main railway station. Turn right under the bridge for the MUSÉE CHAGALL, in the suburbs, so to speak, of Cimiez. Opened in 1973, this elegant museum, with curving inner display walls and cunning overhead and window side-lighting, contains a major collection of paintings on biblical themes, superb stained glass and drawings by Marc Chagall (1889-1985), who passed the last years of his life in a villa nearby.

The heart of Roman Nice, CIMIEZ, like the town by the harbour, fell to a succession of later invaders including the Grimaldis of *Monaco, the counts of Savoy (fourteenth century), the kings of France (1706-44), and Savoy (now the kingdom of Sardinia) in the later eighteenth century, Napoleon (1792-1814) and Sardinia once again before being integrated into France in 1860, when Italian Nizza finally became French Nice. By this time it was a firm favourite with the English. The Promenade des Anglais was built with English money in the 1820s. Late in the century the ageing Queen Victoria was a frequent visitor. Her suite at the Grand Hôtel Excelsior Regina (the former name of the Hôtel Regina) had its own royal chapel.

The Roman arena and the Villa des Arènes with its museums is in a pleasant park dotted with pine trees. The ARÈNES Roman amphitheatre was small by ancient standards, housing only 5,500 spectators; it is less impressive than the third-century baths, the ruined remains of which are in the archaeological site to the south of the VILLA DES

ARÈNES. The archaeological collections on the ground floor comprise artefacts and sculptures excavated on the site, along with jewellery and coins and other Roman, Greek and Etruscan antiquities. On the first floor is the MATISSE MUSEUM, with paintings, drawings and sculptures from all periods of his career as well as furniture and other personal effects. A frequent visitor to Nice and Cimiez, Henri Matisse (1869-1954) died at the Hôtel Regina. The park also has a Franciscan priory with an interesting museum devoted to the order's history and some magnificent works of art in the church.

For OLD NICE return to the Place Massena (bus no. 15). Lunch in one of the nearby cafés or, if you choose, a quick picnic in the Jardin Albert 1er. A stroll along the Quai des États-Unis overlooking the shingle beach brings you to the lofty plateau with the ruins of the old castle demolished by the French early in the eighteenth century. Near the sixteenth-century Tour Bellanda, housing a maritime museum, a lift will take you to the top of the hill for a beautiful view of the town, the Mediterranean and the old Port Lympia.

Alternatively, walk to the Castle Hill through the picturesque streets of the old town. The second turn left off the R. de la Préfecture brings you to the Cathédral Ste Réparate. Next follow the R. Rossetti to the PALAIS LASCARIS. The chief glory of old Nice, this magnificent seventeenth-century Genoese-style mansion has a grand stone staircase, ornate ceilings and period furniture, all well restored. [Continue up the R. Droite for a detour via the Place St François – morning fish market – and R. Pairoliers to the stately, arcaded eighteenth-century Place Garibaldi. The R. Neuve leads to the baroque church of St Martin and St Augustine with a beautiful Pietà by Louis Bréa.]

Turn right from the Palais Lascaris down the R. Droite to the early seventeenth-century Church of St Jacques (imitation of the Gesù, Rome) and the Italian baroque Church of Giaume. Reaching the Quai des États-Unis, turn left for the Castle Hill. After exploring the Old Port return to the Jardin Albert 1er. Before leaving Nice, take a last look at the Promenade des Anglais, one of Europe's most famous seafronts, whose renowned hotels – like the Negresco – still retain their air of luxury and chic.

INDEX